PRENTICE HALL

SCIENCE EXPLORER

Electricity and Magnetism

Prentice
Hall

Needham, Massachusetts
Upper Saddle River, New Jersey
Glenview, Illinois

Electricity and Magnetism

Book-Specific Resources

Student Edition
Annotated Teacher's Edition
Teaching Resources with Color Transparencies
Consumable and Nonconsumable Materials Kits
Guided Reading Audio CDs
Guided Reading Audiotapes
Guided Reading and Study Workbook
Guided Reading and Study Workbook, Teacher's Edition
Lab Activity Videotapes
Science Explorer Videotapes
Science Explorer Web Site at **www.phschool.com**

Program-Wide Resources

Computer Test Bank Book with CD-ROM
How to Assess Student Work
How to Manage Instruction in the Block
Inquiry Skills Activity Book
Integrated Science Laboratory Manual
Integrated Science Laboratory Manual, Teacher's Edition
Interactive Student Tutorial CD-ROM
Prentice Hall Interdisciplinary Explorations
Probeware Lab Manual
Product Testing Activities by Consumer Reports™
Program Planning Guide
Reading in the Content Area with Literature Connections
Resource Pro® CD-ROM (Teaching Resources on CD-ROM)
Science Explorer Videodiscs
Standardized Test Preparation Book
Student-Centered Science Activity Books
Teacher's ELL Handbook: Strategies for English Language Learners

Spanish Resources

Spanish Student Edition
Spanish Guided Reading Audio CDs with Section Summaries
Spanish Guided Reading Audiotapes with Section Summaries
Spanish Science Explorer Videotapes

Science Explorer Student Editions

From Bacteria to Plants

Animals

Cells and Heredity

Human Biology and Health

Environmental Science

Inside Earth

Earth's Changing Surface

Earth's Waters

Weather and Climate

Astronomy

Chemical Building Blocks

Chemical Interactions

Motion, Forces, and Energy

Electricity and Magnetism

Sound and Light

ISBN 0-13-054101-X
4 5 6 7 8 9 10   05 04 03

Cover: The powerful magnets that move this maglev train give it a much higher speed than ordinary trains.

Program Authors

Michael J. Padilla, Ph.D.
Professor
Department of Science Education
University of Georgia
Athens, Georgia

Michael Padilla is a leader in middle school science education. He has served as an editor and elected officer for the National Science Teachers Association. He has been principal investigator of several National Science Foundation and Eisenhower grants and served as a writer of the National Science Education Standards.

As lead author of *Science Explorer,* Mike has inspired the team in developing a program that meets the needs of middle grades students, promotes science inquiry, and is aligned with the National Science Education Standards.

Ioannis Miaoulis, Ph.D.
Dean of Engineering
College of Engineering
Tufts University
Medford, Massachusetts

Martha Cyr, Ph.D.
Director, Engineering
    Educational Outreach
College of Engineering
Tufts University
Medford, Massachusetts

Science Explorer was created in collaboration with the College of Engineering at Tufts University. Tufts has an extensive engineering outreach program that uses engineering design and construction to excite and motivate students and teachers in science and technology education.

Faculty from Tufts University participated in the development of *Science Explorer* chapter projects, reviewed the student books for content accuracy, and helped coordinate field testing.

CHAPTER PROJECT

Book Author

Camille L. Wainwright, Ph.D.
Professor of Science Education
Pacific University
Forest Grove, Oregon

Contributing Writers

Edward Evans
Former Science Teacher
Hilton Central School
Hilton, New York

Mark Illingworth
Teacher
Hollis Public Schools
Hollis, New Hampshire

Thomas L. Messer
Science Teacher
Cape Cod Academy
Osterville, Massachusetts

Thomas R. Wellnitz
Science Teacher
The Paideia School
Atlanta, Georgia

Reading Consultant

Bonnie B. Armbruster, Ph.D.
Department of Curriculum
    and Instruction
University of Illinois
Champaign, Illinois

Interdisciplinary Consultant

Heidi Hayes Jacobs, Ed.D.
Teacher's College
Columbia University
New York City, New York

Safety Consultants

W. H. Breazeale, Ph.D.
Department of Chemistry
College of Charleston
Charleston, South Carolina

Ruth Hathaway, Ph.D.
Hathaway Consulting
Cape Girardeau, Missouri

Tufts University Program Reviewers

Content Reviewers

Teacher Reviewers

Stephanie Anderson
Sierra Vista Junior
High School
Canyon Country, California

John W. Anson
Mesa Intermediate School
Palmdale, California

Pamela Arline
Lake Taylor Middle School
Norfolk, Virginia

Lynn Beason
College Station Jr. High School
College Station, Texas

Richard Bothmer
Hollis School District
Hollis, New Hampshire

Jeffrey C. Callister
Newburgh Free Academy
Newburgh, New York

Judy D'Albert
Harvard Day School
Corona Del Mar, California

Betty Scott Dean
Guilford County Schools
McLeansville, North Carolina

Sarah C. Duff
Baltimore City Public Schools
Baltimore, Maryland

Melody Law Ewey
Holmes Junior High School
Davis, California

Sherry L. Fisher
Lake Zurich Middle
School North
Lake Zurich, Illinois

Melissa Gibbons
Fort Worth ISD
Fort Worth, Texas

Debra J. Goodding
Kraemer Middle School
Placentia, California

Jack Grande
Weber Middle School
Port Washington, New York

Steve Hills
Riverside Middle School
Grand Rapids, Michigan

Carol Ann Lionello
Kraemer Middle School
Placentia, California

Jaime A. Morales
Henry T. Gage Middle School
Huntington Park, California

Patsy Partin
Cameron Middle School
Nashville, Tennessee

Deedra H. Robinson
Newport News Public Schools
Newport News, Virginia

Bonnie Scott
Clack Middle School
Abilene, Texas

Charles M. Sears
Belzer Middle School
Indianapolis, Indiana

Barbara M. Strange
Ferndale Middle School
High Point, North Carolina

Jackie Louise Ulfig
Ford Middle School
Allen, Texas

Kathy Usina
Belzer Middle School
Indianapolis, Indiana

Heidi M. von Oetinger
L'Anse Creuse Public School
Harrison Township, Michigan

Pam Watson
Hill Country Middle School
Austin, Texas

Activity Field Testers

Nicki Bibbo
Russell Street School
Littleton, Massachusetts

Connie Boone
Fletcher Middle School
Jacksonville Beach, Florida

Rose-Marie Botting
Broward County
School District
Fort Lauderdale, Florida

Colleen Campos
Laredo Middle School
Aurora, Colorado

Elizabeth Chait
W. L. Chenery Middle School
Belmont, Massachusetts

Holly Estes
Hale Middle School
Stow, Massachusetts

Laura Hapgood
Plymouth Community
Intermediate School
Plymouth, Massachusetts

Sandra M. Harris
Winman Junior High School
Warwick, Rhode Island

Jason Ho
Walter Reed Middle School
Los Angeles, California

Joanne Jackson
Winman Junior High School
Warwick, Rhode Island

Mary F. Lavin
Plymouth Community
Intermediate School
Plymouth, Massachusetts

James MacNeil, Ph.D.
Concord Public Schools
Concord, Massachusetts

Lauren Magruder
St. Michael's Country
Day School
Newport, Rhode Island

Jeanne Maurand
Glen Urquhart School
Beverly Farms, Massachusetts

Warren Phillips
Plymouth Community
Intermediate School
Plymouth, Massachusetts

Carol Pirtle
Hale Middle School
Stow, Massachusetts

Kathleen M. Poe
Kirby-Smith Middle School
Jacksonville, Florida

Cynthia B. Pope
Ruffner Middle School
Norfolk, Virginia

Anne Scammell
Geneva Middle School
Geneva, New York

Karen Riley Sievers
Callanan Middle School
Des Moines, Iowa

David M. Smith
Howard A. Eyer Middle School
Macungie, Pennsylvania

Derek Strohschneider
Plymouth Community
Intermediate School
Plymouth, Massachusetts

Sallie Teames
Rosemont Middle School
Fort Worth, Texas

Gene Vitale
Parkland Middle School
McHenry, Illinois

Zenovia Young
Meyer Levin Junior
High School (IS 285)
Brooklyn, New York

Contents

Electricity and Magnetism

Activities

AN ELECTRICAL ENGINEER IN OUTER SPACE

Ellen Ochoa was born and raised in California. She earned a doctorate in electrical engineering from Stanford University and became an astronaut in 1991. She has flown on two space-shuttle missions. Currently she is a Spacecraft Communicator, an astronaut at Mission Control who talks with other astronauts while they are in space. She is a talented flute player who has taken her flute with her on the shuttle. She hopes to be aboard more missions in space soon.

When she was studying electricity in school science classes, Ellen Ochoa didn't know that some day her studies would help take her into space. "I just always liked math and science," the California-born Dr. Ochoa says. Today she is an astronaut and has flown on two space-shuttle missions. Trained as an electrical engineer, she is an expert in the uses of electricity. This is the important skill she brings to the astronaut team.

Astronaut Ochoa has worked in the testing and training process for robotics — humanlike machines that can carry out complicated tasks in space. On her shuttle flights, Ellen had the key job of controlling one of these machines, the Remote Manipulator System, or RMS. "The RMS is a robotic arm that reaches out of the spacecraft," she explains. "We use electricity to operate it. The RMS is about 50 feet long. On my flights, we used it to pick up a satellite that was in the shuttle payload bay and put it in orbit. Then a few days later, we'd come back and retrieve the satellite and put it back in the spacecraft cargo area." One of the satellites was used by scientists to gather information about the sun and its effects on Earth. Another was used to study Earth's atmosphere.

"We have a work station with two hand controllers. One is sort of like a joystick on a kid's game. The other is like a square knob that you hold. You push and pull, or move up and down or left and right, to move the electrical RMS arm to the correct position."

Talking with Dr. Ellen Ochoa

◄ Ellen Ochoa training on Earth with the RMS

◄ A satellite in the grasp of the RMS arm of the space shuttle *Atlantis*

This diagram of the RMS arm shows its three joints and mechanical hand (at the right). The arm is about 15 meters long.

Q *How did you become interested in science?*

A I got into science because I liked math. I always enjoyed math and did well at it. I was interested in finding out about all the ways that people could use math. So I studied physics at college. I didn't know until then that I would have a career in science.

Q *Did you follow the space program when you were young?*

A Oh sure. It was a very big thing in the 1960s when I was in elementary school. At the time, the Apollo program was sending astronauts to the moon. But it wasn't until I was in graduate school in electrical engineering that I learned how to apply for the space program and what they were looking for in selecting astronauts.

Q *What happened when you applied to the space program?*

A The first time I applied in 1985 I was not selected. So I tried again in 1990 and was chosen. That's been the case with many astronauts. Persistence is one of our qualities.

Q *How do astronauts use electricity in the space shuttle?*

A We use electrical power for many of the systems on board the shuttle. It's used for the computers and for the sensors and detectors to make sure that the life-support systems are working correctly. Many of our instruments for research use other forms of energy related to electricity, like light or radio waves. We can use these instruments, for instance, to measure the chemicals in the atmosphere that affect climate and weather. And, of course, we use radio for communicating with the ground crew.

Q *Where does the electricity you use come from?*

A We have fuel cells on board. We bring up cryogenic (very cold) oxygen and hydrogen. Then we allow the two chemicals to mix together in the fuel cells. Fuel cells use chemical reactions, like batteries. The chemical reactions in fuel cells produce both electricity and water, which we use on board. We would like to carry up more oxygen and hydrogen fuel cells, to make more electric power. But more fuel cells would mean we could carry less of other things, such as the equipment for the scientific experiments we do.

Q *Are you studying other ways to make electricity?*

A We've had two shuttle flights that experimented with tethered satellites. Basically, the idea was to drag a satellite through space on a tether—a long conducting cable. As the conductor passes through Earth's magnetic field, electric current is generated. Tethered satellites are just at the research stage now.

Ellen Ochoa at the controls of the RMS arm with astronaut Donald R. McMonagle

Ellen Ochoa entertains other crew ▶ members during a flight.

An artist's concept of the space shuttle and tethered satellite

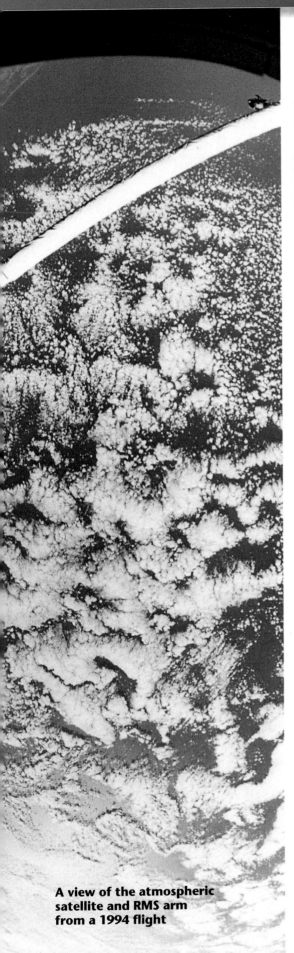

A view of the atmospheric satellite and RMS arm from a 1994 flight

But eventually, we'd like to use power from tethers to move satellites up and down in orbit without using up precious fuel.

Q *What parts of working as an astronaut do you enjoy?*

A I think the whole flight is fun— the launch, viewing Earth from space, and living in weightlessness, although that can be frustrating, too. Doing the activities we've been trained for is hard work, but it's really enjoyable as well. There are a lot of interesting, exciting careers for people with backgrounds in science and math. Being an astronaut is just one of them.

In Your Journal

Ellen talks about persistence, a quality that helped her become an astronaut. Think of a time when you succeeded in doing something after many attempts. Describe what happened. How did persistence and determination help you? Why would these qualities be important for scientists to have?

Magnetism and Electromagnetism

WEB ACTIVITY www.phschool.com

Integrating Earth Science

Electromagnetic Fishing Derby

If you went fishing for cars, what kind of hook would you use—a ship's anchor? Though they resemble giant fishing rods, the cranes used in junkyards to move scrap cars don't use hooks—they use electromagnets.

In this chapter, you will learn what magnets are and how they are used. You will learn about electric current. And you will find out how electric current can be used to produce strong magnets, called electromagnets, that can be turned on and off. As you read the chapter, you will use what you learn to construct an electromagnetic fishing rod. Now go fish!

Your Goal To build an electromagnetic fishing rod that can lift paper clips from one container and drop them into another.

To complete your project you must
- make a model of a fishing rod that has a magnet as its hook
- design an on-off switch for an electromagnet suspended by string from the end of the rod and powered by a single D cell
- modify variables so you can move as many paper clips as possible from one container to another in one minute
- follow the safety guidelines in Appendix A

Get Started Think about fishing rods. Discuss some of their features. Then think about how you could catch and let go of a paper clip with a similar fishing device. Brainstorm ideas for using a magnet as a "hook."

Check Your Progress You'll be working on this project as you study this chapter. To keep your project on track, look for Check Your Progress boxes at the following points.

Section 1 Review, page 21: Make an initial model with a permanent magnet.

Section 3 Review, page 35: Design a switch.

Section 4 Review, page 40: Construct and improve your electromagnet by experimenting with variables.

Wrap Up At the end of the chapter (page 43), you will use your rod to fish alongside classmates in an electromagnetic fishing derby.

A crane uses an electromagnet to move iron and steel in a junkyard.

SECTION
① The Nature of Magnetism

DISCOVER ● **ACTIVITY** ● ● ● ●

What Do All Magnets Have in Common?

1. Obtain a bar magnet and a horseshoe magnet.
2. See how many paper clips you can make stick to different parts of each magnet.
3. Draw a diagram showing the number and location of paper clips on each magnet.

Think It Over

Observing Where does each magnet hold the greatest number of paper clips? What similarities do you observe between the two magnets?

GUIDE FOR READING

◆ How do magnetic poles interact?

◆ What is the shape of magnetic field lines?

◆ How are the domains of a magnet arranged?

Reading Tip As you read, use the headings to make an outline of the main ideas and supporting details about magnetism and electricity.

Imagine zooming along in a train that glides without even touching the ground. You feel no vibration and hear no noise from solid steel tracks. You can just sit back and relax as you speed toward your destination at nearly 400 kilometers per hour.

Are you dreaming? No, you are not. Although you have probably not ridden on such a train, trains capable of floating a few centimeters in air do exist. What makes them float? Believe it or not, magnets make them float.

Figure 1 This Japanese high-speed train is moved by strong magnets instead of wheels. It is called a magnetically levitating train, or maglev train.

Magnets

When you think of magnets, you might think about the magnets that hold notes on your refrigerator. But magnets can also be found in many familiar devices, such as doorbells, televisions, and computers.

Magnets have many modern uses, but they are not new. More than 2000 years ago, people living in a region known as Magnesia discovered an unusual rock. (Magnesia is in Greece.) The rock attracted materials that contained iron. It contained a mineral that we call magnetite. Both the word *magnetite* and the word *magnet* come from the name "Magnesia." **Magnetism** is the attraction of a magnet for another object.

About a thousand years ago, people in other parts of the world discovered another interesting property of magnets. If they allowed the magnetic rock to swing freely from a string, one part of the rock would always point in the same direction. That direction was toward a certain northern star, called the leading star, or lodestar. For this reason, magnetic rocks also became known as lodestones.

Figure 2 Magnetic rocks contain the mineral magnetite.

Magnetic Poles

The magnets with which you are familiar are not found in nature, but they are made to have the same properties as lodestone. Any magnet, no matter what its shape, has two ends, each one called a **magnetic pole.** A pole is the area of a magnet where the magnetic effect is strongest. Just as one end of a piece of magnetite always points toward the north star, one pole of a magnet will also point north and is labeled the north pole. The other pole is labeled the south pole. Two north poles or two south poles are a pair of like poles. A north pole and a south pole are a pair of unlike, or opposite poles.

Figure 3 Modern magnets come in a variety of shapes and sizes. *Classifying How many different shapes of magnets can you identify in the photograph?*

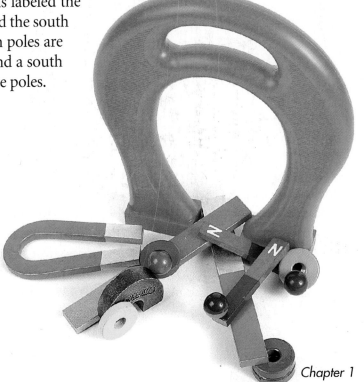

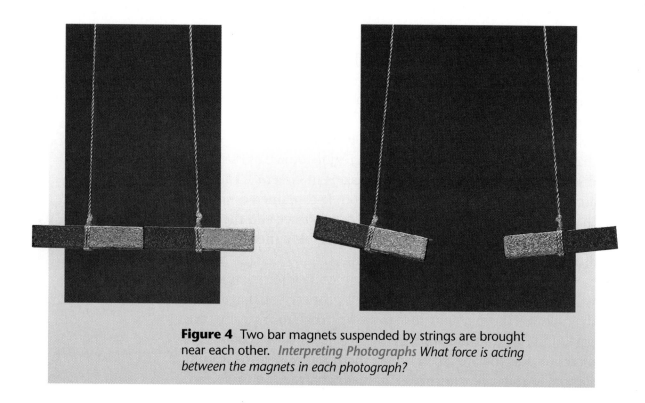

Figure 4 Two bar magnets suspended by strings are brought near each other. *Interpreting Photographs What force is acting between the magnets in each photograph?*

Sharpen your Skills

Observing ACTIVITY

1. Use a pencil to poke a hole in the bottom of a foam cup. Turn the cup upside-down and stand the pencil in the hole.

2. Place two circular magnets on the pencil, so that their like sides are together.

3. Remove the top magnet. Flip it over and replace it on the pencil.

What happens to the magnets in each case? Explain your observations.

Interactions Between Magnetic Poles What happens if you bring two magnets together? The answer depends on how you hold the poles of the magnets. If you bring two north poles together, the magnets push away from each other. The same is true if two south poles are brought together. However, if you bring the north pole of one magnet near the south pole of another, the two magnets attract one another. **Magnetic poles that are alike repel each other and magnetic poles that are unlike attract each other.** Figure 4 shows how two bar magnets interact.

The force of attraction or repulsion between magnetic poles is magnetism. Any material that exerts magnetic forces is considered a magnet.

The maglev train you read about earlier depends on magnetism. Magnets in the bottom of the train and in the guideway on the ground have like poles. Since like poles repel, the two magnets push each other away. The result is that the train car is lifted up, or levitated. Other magnets push and pull the train forward.

Paired Poles What do you think happens if you break a magnet in two? Will you have a north pole in one hand and a south pole in the other? The answer is no. Rather than two separate poles, you will have two separate magnets. Each smaller magnet will be complete with its own north pole and south pole. And if you break those two halves again, you will then have four magnets.

☑ *Checkpoint* *What is a magnetic pole?*

Magnetic Fields

The magnetic force is strongest at the poles of a magnet, but it is not limited to the poles. Magnetic forces are exerted all around a magnet. The region of magnetic force around a magnet is known as its **magnetic field.** Magnetic fields allow magnets to interact without touching.

Figure 5A shows the magnetic field of a bar magnet. The lines, called **magnetic field lines,** map out the magnetic field around a magnet. **Magnetic field lines spread out from one pole, curve around a magnet, and return to the other pole.** The lines form complete loops from pole to pole and never cross.

Although you can't actually see a magnetic field, you can see its effects, as shown in Figure 5B. This photograph shows iron filings sprinkled on a sheet of plastic over a magnet. The magnetic forces act on the iron filings so that they point toward the poles of the magnet. The result is that the iron filings form a pattern similar to the magnetic field lines in Figure 5A.

The iron filings and the diagram are both on flat surfaces. But a magnetic field exists in three dimensions. You can see in Figure 5C that the magnetic field completely surrounds the magnet.

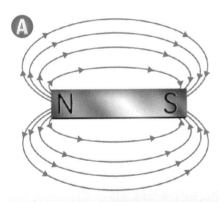

Figure 5 A magnetic field surrounds a magnet.
A. In this diagram, magnetic field lines are shown in red. **B.** You can see the same magnetic field mapped out by iron filings. **C.** Iron filings also show that a magnetic field has three dimensions.

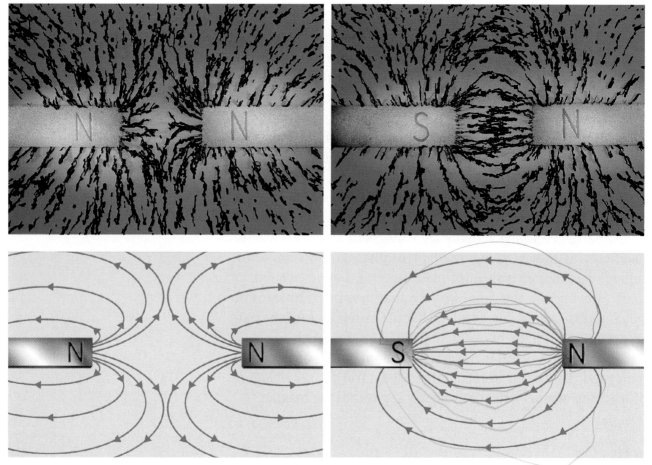

Figure 6 The magnetic field of each bar magnet is altered when two bar magnets are brought together.
Applying Concepts What do these photos and diagrams show about the interaction between magnetic poles?

When the magnetic fields of two or more magnets overlap, the result is a combined field. Figure 6 shows the magnetic fields produced when the poles of two bar magnets are brought near each other.

Inside a Magnet

What happens if you bring a piece of wood, glass, or plastic near a pile of paper clips? Nothing happens. These materials have no effect on the paper clips. But if you bring a bar magnet near the same pile, the paper clips will cling to the magnet. Why do some materials have strong magnetic fields while others do not?

Electron Spin The magnetic properties of a material depend on the structure of its atoms. All matter is made up of atoms. An **atom** is the smallest particle of an element that has the properties of that element. An **element** is one of about 100 basic materials that make up all matter.

The center of every atom is called a **nucleus.** The nucleus contains particles within it. **Protons** are nuclear particles that carry a positive charge. Orbiting the nucleus are other tiny particles called **electrons,** which carry a negative charge. Each of the electrons in an atom acts as if it is spinning as it orbits the nucleus. A moving electron produces a magnetic field. The spinning and orbiting motion of the electrons make each atom a tiny magnet.

Magnetic Domains In most materials the magnetic fields of the atoms point in random directions. The result is that the magnetic fields cancel one another almost entirely. The magnetism of most materials is so weak that you cannot usually detect it.

In certain materials, the magnetic fields of the spinning electrons of many atoms are aligned with one another. A cluster of billions of atoms that all have magnetic fields that are lined up in the same way is known as a **magnetic domain.** The entire domain acts like a bar magnet with a north pole and a south pole.

In a material that is not magnetized, the domains point in random directions as shown in Figure 7. The magnetic fields exerted by some of the domains cancel the magnetic fields exerted by other domains. The result is that the material is not a magnet. **In a magnetized material all or most of the domains are arranged in the same direction.** In other words, the domains are aligned.

Magnetic Materials A material can be a strong magnet if it forms magnetic domains. A material that shows strong magnetic effects is said to be a **ferromagnetic material.** The word *ferromagnetic* comes from the Latin *ferrum*, which means "iron." Iron, nickel, and cobalt are the common ferromagnetic materials. Others include the rare elements samarium and neodymium, which can be made into magnets that are extremely powerful. Some very strong magnets are also made from mixtures, or alloys, of several metals.

Figure 7 The arrows represent the domains of a material. The arrows point toward the north pole of each domain. *Comparing and Contrasting How does the arrangement of domains differ between magnetized iron and unmagnetized iron?*

✓ *Checkpoint How is magnetism related to domains?*

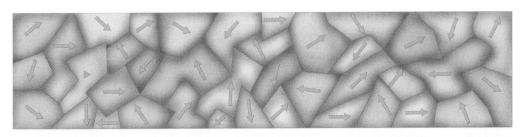

Unmagnetized Iron

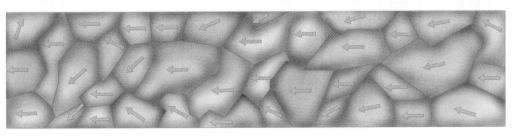

Magnetized Iron

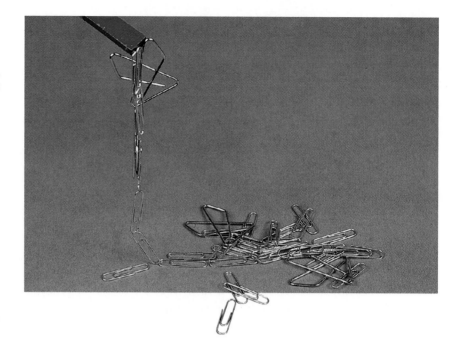

Figure 8 The magnet attracts the metal paper clips. *Applying Concepts How can a paper clip be attracted to a magnet?*

TRY THIS

How Attractive!

You can use iron filings to find out how materials become magnetic.

ACTIVITY

1. Fill a clear plastic tube about two-thirds full with iron filings. Seal the tube.

2. Observe the arrangement of the filings.

3. Rub the tube lengthwise about 30 times in the same direction with one end of a strong magnet.

4. Again observe the arrangement of the filings.

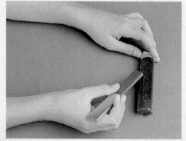

Making Models How do the iron filings in the tube model magnetic domains?

Making Magnets

You know that magnetite exists in nature. The magnets you use everyday, however, are made by people. A magnet can be made from a ferromagnetic material. This is done by placing the unmagnetized material in a strong magnetic field or by rubbing it with one pole of a strong magnet.

If the magnetic field is strong enough, two processes take place. First, the domains that point in the direction of the magnetic field become larger by lining up the fields of neighboring domains. Second, domains that are not pointing in the same direction as the magnetic field rotate toward the magnetic field. The result is that the majority of domains line up in the same direction. With its domains aligned, the material is a magnet.

The ability to make a magnet explains why an unmagnetized object, such as a paper clip, can be attracted to a magnet. Paper clips are made of steel, which is mostly iron. The magnet's field causes domains in the paper clip to line up slightly so that the clip becomes a magnet. Its north pole faces the south pole of the magnet. The paper clip can attract other paper clips for the same reason. After the magnet is removed, however, the domains of the paper clips return to their random arrangements. Thus the paper clips are no longer magnetic.

Some metals, such as the ordinary steel that paper clips are made of, are easy to magnetize but lose their magnetism quickly. Magnets made from these materials are called temporary magnets. Harder metals, such as other types of steel, are more difficult to magnetize but tend to stay magnetized. A magnet made of a material that keeps its magnetism is called a **permanent magnet.**

✓ *Checkpoint* *How does a magnet attract another object?*

Destroying Magnets

Just as paper clips lose their magnetism when their domains become randomly arranged, a permanent magnet can also become unmagnetized. One way is to drop it or strike it hard. If a magnet is hit hard, its domains can be knocked out of alignment. Heating a magnet will also destroy its magnetism. When an object is heated, its particles vibrate faster and more randomly. This makes it more difficult for all the domains to stay lined up. In fact, above a certain temperature a material loses the property of ferromagnetism. The temperature depends on the material.

Breaking Magnets

Now that you know about domains, you can understand why breaking a magnet in half does not result in two pieces that are individual poles. Within the original bar magnet shown in Figure 9, there are many north and south poles facing each other. These poles balance each other.

At the ends of the magnet, there are many poles that are not facing an opposite pole. This produces strong magnetic effects at the north and south poles. If the magnet is cut in half, the domains will still be lined up in the same way. So the shorter pieces will still have strong ends made up of many north or south poles. Figure 9 shows the results of dividing a magnet into four pieces.

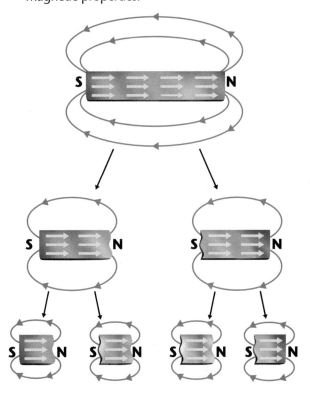

Figure 9 No matter how many times a magnet is cut in half, each piece retains its magnetic properties.

Section 1 Review

1. What happens if you bring together two like poles? Two unlike poles?
2. How are magnetic domains arranged in a magnet? How are they arranged in an unmagnetized object?
3. What parts of an atom produce magnetism?
4. How is a magnet made?
5. **Thinking Critically** **Applying Concepts** Iron filings align with the magnetic field of a bar magnet. What must be happening to the domains in the iron filings in the magnetic field?

CHAPTER PROJECT 1

Check Your Progress
Gather materials for the different parts of your fishing rod. Consider such items as a broom handle, dowel, or meter stick for the rod. You'll also need a string. Draw a basic design for your fishing rod. Make a model of the rod with a permanent magnet. Test how easily you can maneuver your model.

Detecting Fake Coins

S uppose there has been a rash of fake steel coins used in vending machines. The machines may be removed by the owners unless someone can prevent the fake coins from being used. What can you do?

Problem

How can you use a magnet to tell the difference between real and fake coins?

Skills Focus

predicting, inferring

Materials

various coins   craft stick   tape
metric ruler   pencil   protractor
coin-size steel washers
small bar magnet, about 2 cm wide
thin, stiff cardboard, about 25 cm × 30 cm

Procedure

1. Mark a piece of cardboard to show its front, back, top, and bottom.
2. Draw a line lengthwise down the middle of both sides of the cardboard.
3. On the back of the cardboard, draw a line parallel to the first and about 2 cm to the right.
4. Place a magnet vertically about a third of the way down the line you drew in Step 3. Tape the magnet in place.
5. Place a craft stick on the front of the cardboard. The stick's upper end should be about 1 cm to the left of the center line and about 8 cm from the bottom of the cardboard.
6. Tape the stick at an angle, as shown in the photograph.
7. Prop the cardboard against something that will hold it at an angle of about 45°. Predict what will happen when you slide a coin down the front of the cardboard.
8. Place a coin on the center line and slide the coin down the front of the cardboard. (*Hint:* If the coin gets stuck, slowly increase the angle.)
9. Predict what will happen when you slide a steel washer.
10. Test your prediction by sliding a washer down the cardboard. Again, if the washer gets stuck, slowly increase the angle and try again.
11. Once you have reached an angle at which the objects slide easily, send down a randomly mixed group of coins and washers.

Analyze and Conclude

1. What was your prediction from Step 7? Explain your reasoning.
2. What was your prediction from Step 9? Explain your reasoning.
3. Describe how observations made during the lab either supported or did not support your predictions.
4. What is the role of the magnet in this lab?
5. What is the role of the craft stick?
6. Why did you have to use thin cardboard?
7. What can you conclude about the metals from which the coins are made? About the metals in the washers?
8. Why does the steepness of the cardboard affect how the coin separating device works?

9. **Apply** Some Canadian coins contain metals that are attracted to magnets. Would this device be useful in Canada to detect fake coins? Explain your answer.

Getting Involved

Go to a store that has vending machines. Find out who owns the vending machines. Ask the owners if they have a problem with counterfeit coins (sometimes called "slugs"). Ask how they or the makers of the vending machines solve the problem. How is their solution related to the device you built in this lab?

2 Magnetic Earth

DISCOVER .... ACTIVITY ....

Can You Use a Needle to Make a Compass?

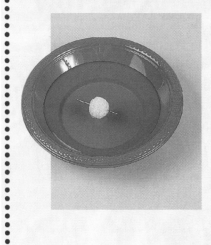

1. ✂ Magnetize a large needle by rubbing it several times in the same direction with one end of a strong bar magnet. Push the needle through a ball of foam or tape it to a small piece of cork.

2. Place a drop of dishwashing soap in a dish of water. Then float the foam or cork in the water. Adjust the needle until it floats horizontally.

3. Allow the needle to stop moving. Which way does it point?

4. Use a local map to determine the direction in which it points.

Think It Over

Observing In what direction did the needle point? Will it always point in the same direction? What does this tell you about Earth?

GUIDE FOR READING

◆ What are the magnetic properties of Earth?

◆ What are the effects of Earth's magnetic field?

Reading Tip As you read, make a table that compares the magnetic fields of Earth and a bar magnet.

When Christopher Columbus sighted land in 1492, he didn't really know what he had found. He was trying to find a shortcut from Europe to India. Where he landed, however, was on an island in the Caribbean Sea just south of the present-day United States. He had no idea that such an island even existed.

In spite of his error, Columbus had successfully followed a course west to the Americas without the help of an accurate map. Instead, Columbus used a compass for navigation. A **compass** is a device that has a magnetized needle that can spin freely. The compass needle usually points north, and as you read you'll find out why.

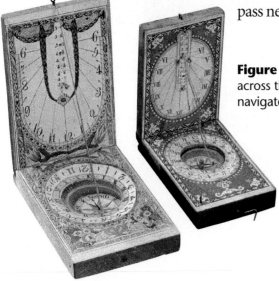

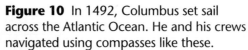

Figure 10 In 1492, Columbus set sail across the Atlantic Ocean. He and his crews navigated using compasses like these.

Figure 11 William Gilbert demonstrates his research to Queen Elizabeth I.

Earth as a Magnet

In the late 1500s, the English physician Sir William Gilbert became interested in compasses. He spoke with several navigators and experimented with his own compass. Gilbert confirmed that a compass always points in the same direction, no matter where you are. But no one knew why.

Gilbert suggested that a compass behaves as it does because Earth acts as a giant magnet. Although many educated people of his time laughed at this idea, Gilbert turned out to be correct. **Earth has an immense magnetic field surrounding it, just as there is a magnetic field around a bar magnet.**

Gilbert believed that the center of Earth contains magnetic rock. Scientists now believe that this is not the case, since Earth's core is too hot for the rock to be solid. Earth's magnetism is still not completely understood. Scientists do know that it is due to the circulation of molten metal (iron and nickel) within Earth's core.

The fact that Earth has a magnetic field explains why a compass works as it does. The poles of the magnetized needle on the compass align themselves with Earth's magnetic field.

Checkpoint **What was Gilbert's new idea about Earth?**

Magnetic Declination

Earth's magnetic poles are not the same as the geographic poles. For example, the magnetic north pole (in northern Canada) is about 1,250 kilometers from the geographic north pole. The geographic north pole is sometimes called true north. The magnetic south pole is located near the coast of Antarctica.

Measuring

1. Use a local map to locate geographic north relative to your school. Mark the direction on the floor with tape or chalk.

2. Use a compass to find magnetic north. Again mark the direction.

3. Use a protractor to measure the number of degrees between the two marks.

Compare the directions of magnetic and geographic north. Is magnetic north to the east or west of geographic north?

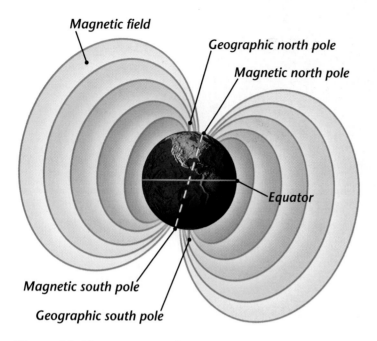

Magnetic field

Geographic north pole

Magnetic north pole

Equator

Magnetic south pole

Geographic south pole

Figure 12 The magnetic poles are not located exactly at the geographic poles.

You can see the difference between the magnetic and geographic poles more clearly by imagining lines that connect each set of poles together. Figure 12 shows that the line connecting Earth's magnetic poles is tipped slightly from Earth's axis—the imaginary line around which Earth rotates.

If you use a compass you have to account for the fact that the geographic and magnetic poles are different. Suppose you could draw a line between you and the geographic north pole. The direction of this line is geographic north. Then imagine a second line between you and the magnetic pole. The angle between these two lines is the angle between geographic north and the north to which a compass needle points. This angle is known as **magnetic declination.**

Magnetic declination differs depending on where you are. Figure 13 shows magnetic declination in various locations in the United States. In North Carolina, for example, a hiker must head about 8 degrees east of the compass reading to get to a place that

Figure 13 Magnetic declination varies with location.
Interpreting Maps What is the magnetic declination where you live?

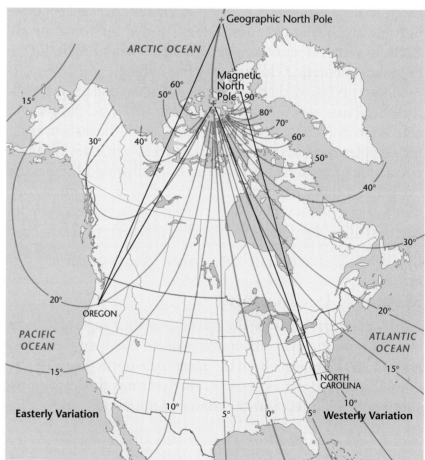

Figure 14 Earth's magnetic field differs from that of a bar magnet due to the solar wind. The solar wind causes the magnetic field to stretch out on the side of Earth experiencing night.

is directly north on a map. A hiker in Oregon would have to head about 20 degrees west of the compass reading.

Magnetic declination changes over time because the magnetic poles move slowly. Between 1580 and 1820, for example, the direction of magnetic north in London changed by 35 degrees.

☑ *Checkpoint* *What is magnetic declination?*

The Magnetosphere

Earth's magnetic field extends into space, which contains electrically charged particles. **Earth's magnetic field affects the movements of electrically charged particles in space. Charged particles also affect Earth's magnetic field.**

Between 1,000 and 25,000 kilometers above Earth's surface are two doughnut-shaped regions called the **Van Allen belts.** They are named after their discoverer, J. A. Van Allen. These regions contain electrons and protons traveling at very high speeds. At one time it was feared the particles would be dangerous for spacecraft passing through them, but this has not been the case.

Other electrically charged particles in space come from the sun. Earth and the other planets experience a solar wind. The **solar wind** is a stream of electrically charged particles flowing at high speeds from the sun. The solar wind pushes against Earth's magnetic field, and surrounds the field, as shown in Figure 14. The region of Earth's magnetic field shaped by the solar wind is called the **magnetosphere.** The solar wind constantly reshapes the magnetosphere as Earth rotates on its axis.

Although most particles in the solar wind cannot penetrate Earth's magnetic field, some particles do. They follow the lines of Earth's magnetic field to the magnetic poles. At the poles the magnetic field lines dip down to Earth's surface.

Spinning in Circles

Which way will a compass point?

1. Place a bar magnet in the center of a sheet of paper.
2. Place a compass about 2 cm beyond the north pole of the magnet. Draw a small arrow showing the direction of the compass needle.
3. Repeat Step 2 at 20 to 30 different positions around the magnet.
4. Remove the magnet and observe the pattern of arrows you drew.

Drawing Conclusions What does your pattern of arrows represent? Do compasses respond only to Earth's magnetic field?

Figure 15 A band of colors called an aurora appears in the sky near the magnetic poles. *Relating Cause and Effect What causes an aurora?*

When charged particles get close to Earth's surface, they interact with atoms in the atmosphere. This causes the atoms to give off light. The result is one of Earth's most spectacular displays—a curtain of shimmering bright light in the atmosphere. A glowing region caused by charged particles from the sun is called an **aurora.** In the northern hemisphere, an aurora is called the Northern Lights, or aurora borealis. In the southern hemisphere, it is called the Southern Lights, or aurora australis.

Effects of Earth's Magnetic Field

You learned that a material such as iron can be made into a magnet by a strong magnetic field. **Since Earth produces a strong magnetic field, Earth itself can make magnets.**

Earth as a Magnet Maker Suppose you leave an iron bar lying in a north-south direction for many years. Earth's magnetic field can attract the domains strongly enough to cause them to line up in the same direction. (Recall that a strong magnetic field can cause the magnetic domains of a ferromagnetic material to increase in size or to line up in the same direction.) To speed the process, you could gently tap on the bar with a hammer. This vibrates the domains and they can then be aligned by the magnetic field.

What objects might be lying in Earth's magnetic field for many years? Consider metal objects or appliances that are left in the same position for many years, such as filing cabinets in your school. Even though no one has tried to make them into magnets, Earth might have done so anyway.

Earth Leaves a Record Earth's magnetic field also acts on rocks that contain magnetic material, such as rock on the ocean floor. The ocean floor is produced from molten material that seeps up through a long crack in the ocean floor, known as the mid-ocean ridge. When the rock is molten, the iron it contains lines up in the direction of Earth's magnetic field. As the rock cools and hardens, the iron is locked in place. This creates a permanent record of the magnetic field.

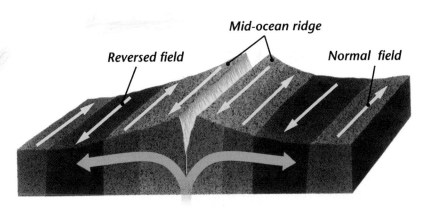

Figure 16 When volcanic lava on the ocean floor hardens into rock, the direction of Earth's magnetic field at that time is permanently recorded.

As scientists studied such rock, they discovered that the direction and strength of Earth's magnetic field has changed over time. Earth's magnetic poles periodically reverse themselves. This last happened about 780,000 years ago.

The yellow arrows in Figure 16 indicate the direction of Earth's magnetic field. Notice that the patterns of bands on either side of the ridge are mirror images. This is because the sea floor spreads apart from the mid-ocean ridge. So rocks farther from the ridge are older than rocks near the ridge. The magnetic record in the rock depends on when the rock was formed.

You might be wondering why Earth's magnetic field changes direction. If so, you're not alone. Scientists have asked the same question. Earth's magnetic field arises from the motion of molten metal in Earth's core. Changes in the flow of that metal result in changes in Earth's magnetic field. But the details of this theory have not been worked out, and so scientists cannot explain why the flow changes. Maybe someday you will be able to shed light on this area.

Section 2 Review

1. How is Earth like a magnet?
2. Compare Earth's geographic poles with its magnetic poles.
3. How does a compass work?
4. What evidence of changes in Earth's magnetic field is found in rocks?
5. **Thinking Critically** **Developing Hypotheses** Some insects and birds have tiny particles of iron in parts of their body that are connected by nerves to their brain. What could be the function of the iron particles?

Science at Home

Explore your home with a compass. Use the compass to discover objects that are magnetized. For example, test the top and bottom of the stove, refrigerator, or a metal filing cabinet. Try metal objects that have been in the same position over a long period of time. Explain why these objects attract or repel a compass needle.

3 Electric Current and Magnetic Fields

DISCOVER ···················· ACTIVITY

Are Magnetic Fields Limited to Magnets?

1. Obtain two wires with the insulation removed from both ends. Each wire should be 20 to 30 cm long.

2. Connect one end of each wire to a socket containing a small light bulb.

3. Connect the other end of one of those wires to a D cell.

4. Place 3 compasses near the wire at any 3 positions. Note the direction in which the compasses are pointing.

5. Center the wire over the compasses. Make sure the compass needles are free to turn.

6. Touch the free end of the remaining wire to the battery. Observe the compasses as current flows through the wire. Move the wire away from the battery, and then touch it to the battery again. Watch the compasses.

Think It Over
Inferring What happened to the compasses? What can you infer about electricity and magnetism?

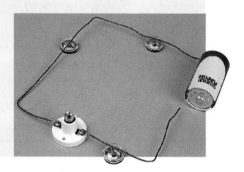

GUIDE FOR READING

◆ How is an electric current related to a magnetic field?

◆ How are conductors different from insulators?

◆ What are the characteristics of an electric circuit?

Reading Tip As you read, use the headings to make an outline.

In 1820, the Danish scientist Hans Christian Oersted (UR sted) was teaching a class at the University of Copenhagen. During his lecture, he allowed electricity to flow through a wire, just as electricity flows through wires to your electrical appliances. When electricity flowed, he noticed that the needle of a compass near the wire changed direction.

Oersted's observations surprised him. He could have assumed that something was wrong with his equipment. Instead, he investigated further. He set up several compasses around a wire. Oersted discovered that whenever he turned on the electricity, the compass needles lined up in a circle around the wire.

Oersted's discovery showed that magnetism and electricity are related. But just how are they related? To find out, you must learn about electric current.

Electric Current

You learned in Section 1 that all matter contains particles called electrons and protons. Electrons and protons have a property called **electric charge.** Electrons are negatively charged, and protons are positively charged.

◄ Oersted's demonstration

B. Compass needles align themselves with the magnetic field of a current moving upward (blue arrow).

C. Compass needles reverse their directions to align with the magnetic field of a current moving downward.

Figure 17 Current in a wire affects a compass needle.
A. With no current flowing, the compass needles all point to magnetic north.

When electric charges flow through a wire or similar material, they create an electric current. **Electric current** is the flow of charge through a material. The amount of charge that passes through the wire in a unit of time is the rate at which electric current flows. The unit of current is the ampere (amp or A), named for André-Marie Ampère. You will often see the name of the unit shortened to "amp." The number of amps tells the amount of charge flowing past a given point each second.

What does all of this have to do with magnetism? **An electric current produces a magnetic field.** The lines of the magnetic field produced by a current in a straight wire are in the shape of circles with the wire at their center. You can see in Figure 17 that compasses placed around a wire line up with the magnetic field. The iron filings in Figure 18 map out the same field. The direction of the current determines the direction of the magnetic field. If the current is reversed, the magnetic field reverses as well. You can see this from the compasses in Figure 17C.

Moving Charge and Magnetism

Ampère carried out many experiments with electricity and magnetism. He hypothesized that all magnetism is a result of circulating charges. Atoms, for example, can become magnets because of the motion of the electrons. Based on modern knowledge of magnetism, Ampère's hypothesis is correct. All magnetism is caused by the movement of charges.

Checkpoint *What particles have electric charge?*

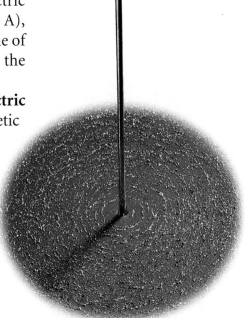

Figure 18 Iron filings show the field lines around a wire that carries a current.
Observing What is the shape of the field lines?

Electric Circuits

An electric current will not flow automatically through every wire. Current flows only through electric circuits. An **electric circuit** is a complete path through which electric charges can flow. All electrical devices, from toasters to radios to electric guitars and televisions, contain electric circuits.

All circuits have the same basic features. **First, a circuit has a source of electrical energy.** Energy is the ability to do work. **Second, circuits have devices that are run by electrical energy.** A radio, a computer, a light bulb, and a refrigerator are all devices that convert electrical energy into another form of energy. A light bulb, for example, converts electrical energy to electromagnetic energy (it gives off light) and thermal energy (it gives off heat).

Third, electric circuits are connected by conducting wires and a switch. In order to describe a circuit, you can draw a circuit diagram. *Exploring Electric Circuits* on the next page shows a circuit diagram along with the symbols that represent the parts of the circuit. As you read, identify the parts of a circuit and their symbols.

Conductors and Insulators

Electric current flows through metal wires. Will it also flow through plastic or paper? The answer is no. Electric current does not flow through every material.

Electric currents move freely through materials called **conductors.** Metals, such as copper, silver, iron, and aluminum, are good conductors. **In a conductor, some of the electrons are only loosely bound to their atoms.** These electrons, called conduction electrons, are able to move throughout the conductor. As these electrons flow through a conductor, they form an electric current.

Did you ever wonder why a light goes on the instant you flip the switch? How do the electrons get to your lamp from the electric company so fast? The answer is that electrons are not created and sent to you when you flip a switch. They are present all along in the conductors that make up the circuit. When you flip the switch, conduction electrons at one end of the wire are pulled while those at the other end are pushed. The result is a continuous flow of electrons as soon as the circuit is completed.

Insulators are a different kind of material in which charges are not able to move freely. **The electrons in an insulator are bound tightly to their atoms and do not flow easily.** Examples of insulators are rubber, glass, sand, plastic, and wood.

Figure 19 Charges behave like the chairs on a ski lift. Charges in all parts of a conducting wire begin to flow at the same time.

☑ *Checkpoint* *What moves freely in a conductor?*

EXPLORING Electric Circuits

Electric circuits are all around you. They are so common that you probably don't think about them. An electric circuit has several basic features.

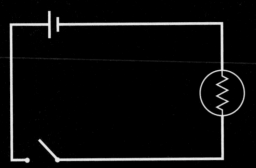

This circuit diagram represents the circuit shown in the photograph. Special symbols are used for the parts of the circuit.

Circuit Symbols

 Switch

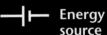 Energy source

 Resistor

Battery
A source of electrical energy makes charges move around a circuit.

Resistor
A device such as a light bulb, appliance, or computer converts electrical energy to another form. Such a device is called a resistor.

Switch
A switch is used to open and close the circuit. When the switch is closed, the electric circuit is complete. When the switch is open, the circuit is broken. Charges cannot flow through a broken path.

Figure 20 Electric current passes through the tungsten filament of a light bulb. As it resists the flow of charge, the filament heats up until it glows.

Classifying

Gather several objects such as keys, foam, pencil lead, aluminum foil, wax paper, and paper clips. Predict which items will be conductors.

1. Obtain three 10-cm wires with the insulation removed from both ends.

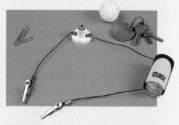

2. Construct a circuit like the one shown. Use the wires, a light bulb, a D cell, and two alligator clips.

3. Insert a test object between the two clips. Observe the light bulb. Repeat the test with each of the other objects.

Which objects are conductors? Which are insulators? How do you know?

Electrical Resistance

As charges flow through a circuit, they pass through resistors. A **resistor** uses electrical energy as it interferes with, or resists, the flow of charge. The opposition to the movement of charges flowing through a material is called **resistance.**

The resistance of a material depends on its atomic structure. Think about walking through a room with people in it. If the people are spread out, you can easily walk through the room without bumping into anyone. But if the people are crowded together, you will bump into people as you move through the room. In a similar way, an electron collides with particles in a material. During each collision, some of the electron's energy is converted to thermal energy (felt as heat) or electromagnetic energy (seen as light). The more collisions, the more electrical energy is converted.

The Light Bulb Thomas Edison used resistance when he was

INTEGRATING TECHNOLOGY developing his electric light bulb. Edison experimented with many materials. He needed one that would conduct electric current, but would offer enough resistance to make the material heat up and glow. Edison tried copper wires, silk fibers, shredded corn husks, and even human hair. He had some success with cotton threads, then later he settled on charcoal made from bamboo slivers. Eventually, bamboo was replaced with wire made from tungsten. Tungsten is a metal that can get hot enough to glow without melting.

Figure 21 The magnetic field of the superconductor repels the magnetic cube. Thus the cube floats above the superconductor, much like the maglev train in Section 1.

Superconductors Scientists have discovered that some materials become superconductors at very low temperatures. A **superconductor** is a material that has no electrical resistance. A superconductor is very different from an ordinary conductor. Without resistance, a current flows through a superconductor with no loss of energy. Using superconducting wires would reduce wasted electrical energy and make electrical devices more efficient. Superconductors strongly repel magnets, as you can see in Figure 21. But their use as magnets is limited. A strong magnetic field destroys the superconductivity of a substance, turning it back into an ordinary conductor!

The greatest problem with superconductors is that very low temperatures are required. However, new materials have been found that become superconducting at higher temperatures. At the present time, researchers are working to make superconductors practical.

 ## Section 3 Review

1. Are electricity and magnetism related? Explain.
2. What is the difference between a conductor and an insulator? Give an example of each.
3. What is an electric circuit?
4. **Thinking Critically Relating Cause and Effect** Why does a compass needle move when placed near a wire carrying an electric current? What do you think happens to the compass needle when the circuit is shut off?

Check Your Progress
CHAPTER PROJECT 1
Construct an electric circuit for your fishing rod with a D cell and a piece of insulated wire about 12 meters long. Your fishing rod will need a switch. Making a switch is a matter of closing a circuit. One way to do this is to tape one end of your wire to one end of the battery and then to touch the other end of the wire to the other end of the battery. Think of a less awkward way of controlling the fishing rod.

Real-World Lab

BUILD A FLASHLIGHT

Imagine that you are camping in a forest. You hear noises outside your tent; something is rustling and bumping around nearby. At this moment, there is one device you might *really* appreciate having—a flashlight. Have you ever examined one to determine how it works?

Problem

How can you build a working flashlight?

Skills Focus

making models, observing, inferring

Materials

one cardboard tube
flashlight bulb
paper cup
scissors
one D cell
aluminum foil
duct tape

2 lengths of wire, about 10 cm, with the insulation stripped off about 2 cm at each end
1 length of wire, 15–20 cm, with the insulation stripped off each end

Procedure

1. Check that the D cell fits inside the cardboard tube. Make two holes in the side of the tube about 2–3 cm apart. The holes should be near the middle of the tube.
2. Use duct tape to connect a 10-cm wire to each terminal of the battery. Touch the other ends of the wires to a flashlight bulb in order to find where to connect them. (*Hint:* Most bulbs have a bottom contact and a side contact. If there is no obvious side contact, try touching the metal on the side of the base.)

3. Line a paper cup with aluminum foil. Use a pencil to poke a hole in the bottom of the paper cup. The hole should be slightly smaller than the bulb, but large enough to allow the base of the bulb through.
4. Insert the base of the light bulb through the hole. Be sure the bulb fits securely.
5. Pass the long wire through one of the holes in the tube. Tape it to the inside of the tube, leaving about 2 cm outside the tube. The other end should reach the end of the tube.
6. Place the battery in the tube. Pass the wire attached to the bottom of the battery through the other hole in the tube. (Make sure the two wires outside the tube can touch.)
7. Make a sling from duct tape to hold the battery inside the tube.

8. Attach the wires from the end of the tube to the contact points on the bulb.

9. Tape the cup on top of the tube, keeping all connections tight.

10. Touch the two free ends of the wires together to see if the bulb lights. If it doesn't, check to be sure all connections are taped together securely.

Analyze and Conclude

1. What is the purpose of lining the cup with aluminum foil?

2. Does it matter which way the battery is placed in the tube? Explain.

3. Why does the bulb have to be connected at two points in order for it to light?

4. How could you make your flashlight brighter? How could you make it more rugged?

5. Compare your flashlight to a manufactured one. Explain the differences.

6. **Apply** Design a more convenient switch for your flashlight. You may want to use materials such as paper clips, brass fasteners, or aluminum foil. Have your teacher approve your switch design and then build and test the switch.

Getting Involved

People use different types of flashlights for different purposes. Some are narrow and flexible while others are wide and sturdy. Compare several different flashlights. Describe the flashlights. Note the type and number of batteries required, the type of switch used, and any other features that you observe. Suggest useful applications for each flashlight. Then design a new flashlight based on a need that you observe.

How Do You Turn a Magnet On and Off?

1. Wind one meter of wire tightly around an iron nail so that you have at least 25 turns. Leave about 15 centimeters of wire on each end.

2. Attach one end of the wire to one terminal of a D cell.

3. Briefly touch the other end of the wire to the other terminal of the D cell. **CAUTION:** *Do not leave the switch closed for more than two or three seconds at a time. The wire will heat up.*

4. With the circuit complete, bring a paper clip near the nail.

5. Add paper clips one at a time and repeat Steps 3 and 4.

Think It Over

Forming Operational Definitions The device you constructed is called an electromagnet. How does it compare with a bar magnet? Based on your observations, define "electromagnet."

GUIDE FOR READING

◆ What are the characteristics of an electromagnet?

Reading Tip Before you read, preview the illustrations. Write down any questions you have about the illustrations. Answer them as you read the section.

You learned in Section 3 that a current in a wire creates a magnetic field around the wire. By turning the current on and off, you can turn the magnetic field on and off. So by using an electric current to create a magnet, you produce a magnetic field that you can control.

Solenoids

The magnetic field around a current-carrying wire forms a cylinder around the wire. If the wire is twisted into a loop, the magnetic field lines become bunched up inside the loop. You can see this by looking at the iron filings in Figure 22. The strength of the

Figure 22 The magnetic field around a loop of wire bunches up in the center.

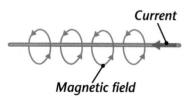

Current

Magnetic field

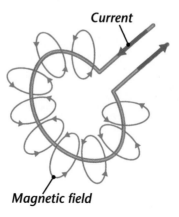

Current

Magnetic field

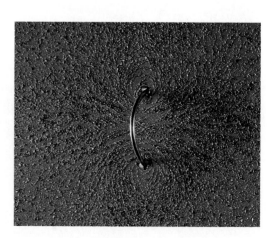

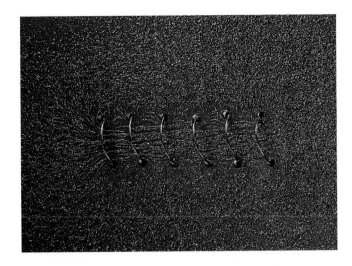

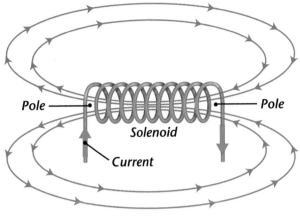

Figure 23 The magnetic field around a solenoid resembles that of a bar magnet. *Comparing and Contrasting How is a solenoid different from a bar magnet?*

magnetic field increases as the number of loops is increased. If the wire is bent into a second loop, the concentration of magnetic field lines within the loop is twice as great.

By winding a current-carrying wire into a coil you have strengthened the magnetic field in the center of the coil. The two ends of the coil act like poles. The iron filings around the loops of wire in Figure 23 line up much as they would around a bar magnet. A current-carrying coil of wire with many loops is called a **solenoid.** A solenoid creates a magnetic field that can be turned on and off by switching the current on and off. The north and south poles change with the direction of the current.

Multiplying Magnetism

If a ferromagnetic material such as iron is placed inside a solenoid, the magnetic field is increased. Recall how a ferromagnetic material acts. When iron is placed within the solenoid's magnetic field, it becomes a magnet as well. A solenoid with a ferromagnetic core is called an **electromagnet.** The temporary magnetic field of an electromagnet is produced by the current in the wire and the magnetized core. The overall magnetic field can be hundreds or thousands of times stronger than the magnetic field produced by the current alone. **An electromagnet is a strong magnet that can be turned on and off.**

An electromagnet is ideal for lifting heavy pieces of scrap metal. Have you ever seen stacks of junked cars? The flattened auto bodies are shredded into small metal fragments. The iron and steel fragments are picked up by a huge electromagnet on a crane. When the switch is turned on, current flows and the electromagnet lifts the metallic scrap and the crane moves it. When the switch is turned off, the pieces of scrap fall from the magnet.

☑ *Checkpoint* What is a solenoid?

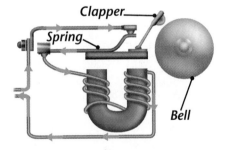

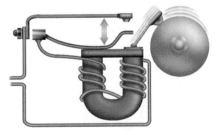

Figure 24 A solenoid is used to ring an alarm bell. When current flows through the circuit, the coil acts as a magnet. The strip of iron on the spring is attracted to the electromagnet and the clapper strikes the bell. At the same time, the spring opens the circuit and stops the current. The spring returns the clapper to its resting position.

Increasing the Strength of an Electromagnet

There are a number of ways you can increase the strength of an electromagnet's field. You can increase the current in the solenoid. You can add more loops of wire to the solenoid. You can wind the coils of the solenoid closer together. Also, you can increase the strength of an electromagnet by using a stronger ferromagnetic material for the core.

Recording Information

 INTEGRATING TECHNOLOGY When you record information on audiotapes, videotapes, computer disks, or credit cards, you are using electromagnets. Think about recording your voice with a tape recorder. When you talk into a microphone, the vibrations of your voice are changed into an electric current that varies with your voice. That current is used in an electromagnet in the recording head of the tape recorder to produce a magnetic field. Since the current changes, the magnetic field of the electromagnet changes as well.

A recording tape consists of a plastic ribbon coated with a thin layer of metal powder. The metal particles of the powder are magnetized by the magnetic field of the electromagnet in the recording head. As the tape moves past the electromagnet, the metal particles are magnetized more or less by the electromagnet. The strength of magnetization of the particles changes with the changing strength of the magnetic field. The magnetic pattern in the tape becomes a code for your voice. When you play the tape back, the code is converted back into sound. In a similar way, electromagnets are used to record images and sounds on videotape and all sorts of information on computer disks.

Figure 25 A magnified photograph shows a pattern of magnetic domains on a cassette tape.

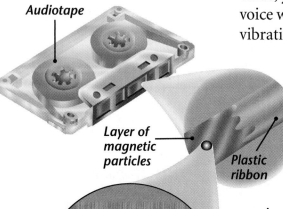

Audiotape

Layer of magnetic particles

Plastic ribbon

Magnified photograph of tape

Section 4 Review

1. Describe an electromagnet in your own words.
2. How is an electromagnet different from a permanent magnet?
3. What are some uses for electromagnets?
4. **Thinking Critically** **Predicting** Will bringing a strong magnet near a computer disk or videotape cause damage to the recorded information? Explain.

Check Your Progress

CHAPTER PROJECT 1

Construct an electromagnet by wrapping a length of insulated wire around one or more iron nails. Attach the ends of the wire to the circuit containing your switch. Test your electromagnet by dipping it into a pile of paper clips to see how many it can pick up at one time. Experiment with the strength of your electromagnet by changing one variable at a time.

CHAPTER 1 STUDY GUIDE

SECTION 1 The Nature of Magnetism

Key Ideas

◆ Unlike magnetic poles attract; like magnetic poles repel.
◆ A magnetic field is a region around a magnet in which magnetic attraction acts.
◆ Magnetic domains are regions in which the magnetic fields of atoms are aligned.
◆ In a magnetized material, most of the domains are lined up in the same direction.

Key Terms

magnetism   nucleus
magnetic pole   proton
magnetic field   electron
magnetic field lines   magnetic domain
atom   ferromagnetic material
element   permanent magnet

SECTION 2 Magnetic Earth

INTEGRATING EARTH SCIENCE

Key Ideas

◆ Earth has a north magnetic pole and a south magnetic pole.
◆ A compass can be used to find directions because its needle lines up with Earth's magnetic poles.
◆ Earth's magnetic poles are not at exactly the same locations as the geographic poles.
◆ The magnetosphere is the magnetic field of Earth as shaped by the solar wind.

Key Terms

compass   solar wind
magnetic declination   magnetosphere
Van Allen belts   aurora

SECTION 3 Electric Current and Magnetic Fields

Key Ideas

◆ Electric current is electric charge in motion.
◆ An electric current produces a magnetic field.
◆ Electric charges flow freely through materials called conductors but not through insulators.
◆ Resistance is the opposition to the movement of charges flowing through a material.

Key Terms

electric charge   insulator
electric current   resistor
electric circuit   resistance
conductor   superconductor

SECTION 4 Electromagnets

Key Ideas

◆ A solenoid creates a magnetic field by means of a current flowing through a coil of wire.
◆ The strength of an electromagnet depends on the amount of current, the number of turns of wire in the coil, how close together the turns of wire are, and the type of magnetic core.

Key Terms

solenoid   electromagnet

Organizing Information

Concept Map Copy the concept map about magnetism onto a separate sheet of paper. Then complete it and add a title. (For more on concept maps, see the Skills Handbook.)

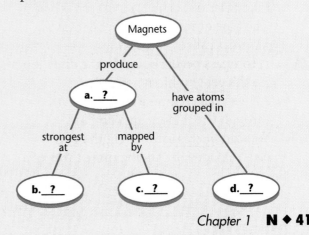

Reviewing Content

 For more review of key concepts, see the Interactive Student Tutorial CD-ROM.

Multiple Choice

Choose the letter of the answer that best completes each statement.

1. The region in which magnetic forces act is called a
   a. line of force.   b. pole.
   c. magnetic field.   d. field of attraction.
2. An example of a ferromagnetic material is
   a. plastic.   b. wood.
   c. copper.   d. iron.
3. The person who first suggested that Earth behaves as a magnet was
   a. Ampère.
   b. Oersted.
   c. Gilbert.
   d. Columbus.
4. The region in which Earth's magnetic field is found is called the
   a. atmosphere.
   b. stratosphere.
   c. aurora.
   d. magnetosphere.
5. A coil of current-carrying wire with an iron core is called a(an)
   a. ferromagnet.
   b. electromagnet.
   c. compass.
   d. maglev.

True or False

If the statement is true, write true. If it is false, change the underlined word or words to make the statement true.

6. Like poles of magnets <u>repel</u> each other.
7. The type of magnetic mineral found in nature is called <u>platinum</u>.
8. A compass needle points in the direction of Earth's <u>geographic</u> north pole.
9. An electric circuit is a complete path through which <u>domains</u> can flow.
10. You can <u>increase</u> the strength of an electromagnet by adding more turns of a wire to it.

Checking Concepts

11. Explain why you are not left with one north pole and one south pole if you break a magnet in half. Draw a diagram to support your answer.
12. How does a material become a magnet?
13. How does Earth act like a magnet?
14. What is an aurora? How is it produced?
15. Why does a compass needle change direction when it is placed near a current-carrying wire?
16. Draw a simple electric circuit. Label and define the basic parts.
17. How is a conductor different from an insulator? Give two examples of each.
18. **Writing to Learn** Did you ever think of a chore that would be much easier if you only had some futuristic device? Here's your chance. Describe a task that you would like to make easier. Then think about how you could use an electromagnet to carry out the task. Be creative in describing your design.

Thinking Critically

19. **Problem Solving** Cassia borrowed her brother's magnet. When she returned it, it was barely magnetic. What might Cassia have done to the magnet?
20. **Comparing and Contrasting** What is the difference between a magnetized iron bar and an unmagnetized one?
21. **Drawing Conclusions** Why might an inexperienced explorer get lost using a compass?
22. **Inferring** A compass points north until a bar magnet is brought next to it. The compass needle is then attracted or repelled by the magnet. What inference can you make about the strengths of the magnetic fields of Earth and the bar magnet?
23. **Relating Cause and Effect** Why does opening a switch in an electric circuit stop the flow of current?
24. **Applying Concepts** How are the uses of an electromagnet different from those of a permanent bar magnet?

Applying Skills

Use the illustration of four electromagnets to answer Questions 25–27.

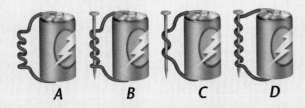

A   B   C   D

25. **Predicting** Will device A or B produce a stronger magnetic field? Will device B or C produce a stronger magnetic field? Explain your choices.

26. **Controlling Variables** Can you tell which electromagnet is the strongest of the four? Explain why or why not.

27. **Designing Experiments** Without changing the number of turns of wire, how could you change the strength of each electromagnet?

Project Wrap Up Test your final electromagnet. Cut the tops off two empty plastic milk containers. Practice moving paper clips from one container to the other until you are ready for a "fishing" competition. After your teacher gives you a one-minute opportunity to fish, compare the most successful designs in the class.

Reflect and Record In your journal, describe the features of other students' designs that worked well. Which switch designs were easiest to operate? What contributed to making the strongest magnets?

Test Preparation

Use these questions to prepare for standardized tests.

Read the passage. Then answer Questions 28–30.

Substances can be classified according to their ability to conduct electric charges. Those that conduct charges well are conductors, and those that do not are insulators.

Whether a substance is classified as a conductor or an insulator depends on how tightly the electrons are bound to the atoms of the substance. Outer electrons of the atoms in a metal, for example, are not tightly bound to the nuclei of particular atoms. Instead, they are free to roam in the material. This makes metals good conductors. The electrons in other materials, such as rubber, plastic, and glass, are tightly bound and remain with particular atoms. These materials are insulators.

28. What is this passage mostly about?
   a. how electric current flows through materials
   b. the characteristics of conductors and insulators
   c. the difference between atoms and electrons
   d. how atoms move in different materials

29. Conductors are different from insulators in that they
   a. have electrons that are free to move within the material.
   b. contain more electrons.
   c. contain more atoms.
   d. are missing some electrons.

30. Based on the passage, which substance do you think might be used to cover electrical wires in a building?
   a. steel   b. copper
   c. plastic   d. aluminum

WEB ACTIVITY
www.phschool.com

Cause for Alarm

A irplane pilots rely on instruments to tell them about all parts of an airplane. The instruments are connected to the rest of the airplane by electric circuits. In this chapter, you will learn about electric charges and how they are involved in static electricity and current electricity. You will also learn about types of current and types of circuits, and how to use electricity safely.

As you work on this chapter project, you will choose an event, such as the opening or closing of a door or window, and design a circuit that alerts you when the event happens.

Your Goal To construct an alarm circuit that will light a bulb in response to some event.

Your circuit must

- ◆ be powered by one or two D cells
- ◆ have a switch that detects your chosen event
- ◆ turn on a light when the switch is closed
- ◆ follow the safety guidelines in Appendix A

Get Started How can you design a switch that detects some event? Brainstorm with your classmates about ways to make two pieces of a conductor come in contact. Make a list of the different ideas your group comes up with.

Check Your Progress You'll be working on this project as you study this chapter. To keep your project on track, look for Check Your Progress boxes at the following points.

Section 2 Review, page 61: Design a detector switch to complete your circuit when the event happens.

Section 3 Review, page 67: Build an alarm circuit completed by your detector switch.

Wrap Up At the end of this chapter (page 75), you'll demonstrate your alarm circuit.

Electric current lights the
instruments in an airplane
and also the runway ahead.

SECTION
1 Electric Charge and Static Electricity

You're in a hurry to get dressed for school, but you can't find one of your socks. You quickly head for the pile of clean laundry. You've gone through everything, but where's the sock? The dryer couldn't have really destroyed it, could it? Oh no, there it is. Your sister has found the sock stuck to one of her shirts. What makes clothes stick together? The explanation has to do with tiny electric charges.

Types of Electric Charge

The charged parts of atoms are electrons and protons. As you have learned, protons and electrons are charged particles. When two protons come close, they push one another apart. In other words, they repel each other. But if a proton and an electron come close, they attract one another.

Why do protons repel protons but attract electrons? The reason is that they have different types of charge. Protons and electrons have opposite charges. The charge on the proton is

Figure 1 The interaction of electric charges is making this girl's hair stand on end.

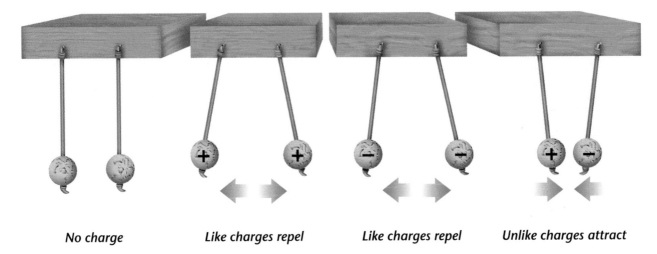

| No charge | Like charges repel | Like charges repel | Unlike charges attract |

called positive (+), and the charge on the electron is called negative (−). The names positive and negative were given to charges by Benjamin Franklin in the 1700s. They have been used by scientists ever since.

Figure 2 Charged objects exert forces on each other. They can either attract or repel.
Interpreting Diagrams What is the rule for the interaction of electric charges?

Interactions Between Charges

The two types of charges interact in specific ways. **Charges that are the same repel each other. Charges that are different attract each other.**

Does this sound familiar to you? This rule is the same as the rule for interactions between magnetic poles. Recall that magnetic poles that are alike repel each other and magnetic poles that are different attract each other.

There is one important thing about electric charges that is different from magnetic poles. Recall that magnetic poles do not exist alone. Whenever there is a south pole, there is always a north pole. Electric charges can exist alone. In other words, a negative charge can exist without a positive charge.

☑ *Checkpoint* How are the interactions between electric charges similar to the interactions between magnetic poles?

Electric Fields

Just as magnetic poles exert their forces over a distance, so do electric charges. An electric charge exerts a force through the **electric field** that surrounds the charge. An electric field extends outward from every charged particle.

When a charged particle is placed in the electric field of another charged particle, it is either pushed or pulled. It is pushed away if the two charges are the same. It is pulled toward the other charge if the two charges are different.

Sharpen your Skills

Drawing Conclusions

ACTIVITY

1. Tear tissue paper into small pieces, or cut circles out of it with a hole punch.
2. Run a plastic comb through your hair several times.
3. Place the comb close to, but not touching, the tissue paper pieces. What do you observe?

What can you conclude about the electric charges on the comb and the tissue paper?

Electric Fields Around Single Charges You will recall using magnetic field lines to picture a magnetic field in an earlier chapter. In a similar way, you can use electric field lines to visualize the electric field. Electric field lines are drawn with arrows to show the direction of the force on a positive charge.

The electric fields in Figure 3A are strongest where the lines are closest together. You can see that the strength of the electric field is greatest near the charged particle. The field decreases as you move away from the charge.

Electric Fields Around Multiple Charges When there are two or more charges, the resulting electric field is altered. The electric fields due to the individual charges combine. Figure 3B shows the electric fields from two sets of charges.

☑ *Checkpoint* *Where is an electric field strongest?*

Static Charge

If matter consists of charged particles that produce electric fields, why aren't you attracted to or repelled by every object around you—your book, your desk, or your pen? The reason is that each atom has an equal number of protons and electrons. And the size, or magnitude, of the charge on an electron is the same as the size of the charge on a proton. So each positive charge is balanced by a negative charge. The charges cancel out and the object as a whole is neutral. As a result there is no overall electrical force.

Figure 3 Electric charges can attract or repel one another.
A. The arrows show that a positive charge repels another positive charge. A negative charge attracts a positive charge. **B.** When two charged particles come near each other, the electric fields of both particles are altered.

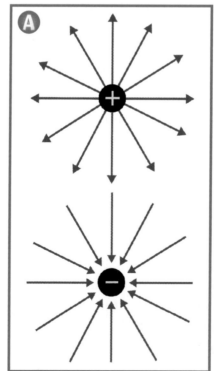

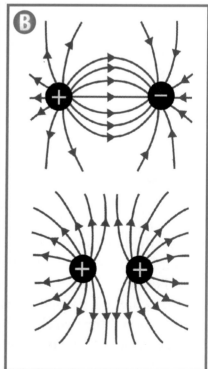

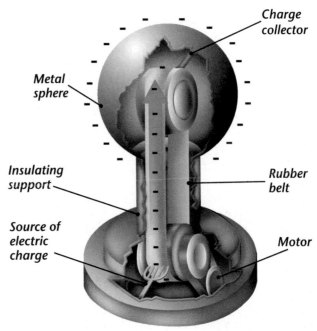

Figure 4 A Van de Graaff generator produces static electricity. Electrons are carried up a rubber belt and are transferred to the metal sphere. The charge built up on the sphere is enough to send a spark several meters through the air.

Charged Objects Protons are bound tightly in the center of an atom, but electrons can sometimes leave their atoms. Whether or not an electron will move depends on the material. Atoms in insulators, such as wood, rubber, plastic, and glass, hold their electrons tightly. Atoms in conductors, such as gold, silver, copper, and aluminum, hold some of their electrons loosely. These electrons move freely from atom to atom within the material.

A neutral object can become charged by gaining or losing electrons. If an object loses electrons, it is left with more protons (positive charge) than electrons (negative charge). Thus the object is positively charged overall. If, instead, an object gains electrons, it has more electrons than protons. Thus it has an overall negative charge.

The buildup of charges on an object is called **static electricity.** Static electricity behaves quite differently from electric currents. In an electric current, charges move continuously. **In static electricity, charges build up, but they do not flow.**

Transferring Charge Exactly how do charges build up? Charges must be transferred from one object to another. There are three methods by which charges are transferred: friction, conduction, and induction. **Friction** is the transfer of electrons from one object to another by rubbing. **Conduction** is the transfer of electrons from a charged object to another object by direct contact.

Induction is the movement of electrons to one part of an object caused by the electric field of another object. The three methods of transferring charge are illustrated in *Exploring Static Electricity*.

Keep in mind that charges are not created or destroyed. If an object gives up electrons, another object gains those electrons. Electrons are only transferred from one location to another. This is known as the law of **conservation of charge.**

Static Cling Static electricity explains why clothes stick together in the clothes dryer. In a dryer, different fabrics rub together. Electrons from one fabric rub off onto another. In this way, the clothes become charged. A positively charged sock might then be attracted to a negatively charged shirt—the clothes stick together.

Your clothes are less likely to stick together if you use a fabric softener sheet. These sheets add a thin coating to your clothes as they bounce around in the dryer. The coating prevents electrons from rubbing off the clothing, so the clothes don't become charged.

Can you think of situations in which you might want to increase static electricity? Think about wrapping leftover food in plastic wrap. Plastic wrap picks up a charge when you unroll it. Since plastic is an insulator, the charge cannot easily move off it. So the wrap keeps its charge. When you place the plastic wrap on a container, it charges the edges of the container by induction. The force between the opposite charges on the wrap and the container causes the wrap to cling.

Static electricity allows you to make copies quickly. In a photocopier, a drum is given a negative static charge that is the image of the page to be copied. This charged image picks up positively charged particles of a very fine black powder. The drum then rolls against a negatively charged piece of paper, and the powder is transferred to the paper. Finally, the paper is heated to melt the powder, and the powder sticks to the paper.

☑ *Checkpoint* *What is the law of conservation of charge?*

Static Discharge

An object that gains a static charge doesn't hold the charge forever. Electrons tend to move, returning the object to its neutral condition. **When a negatively charged object and a positively charged object are brought together, electrons move until both objects have the same charge.** The loss of static electricity as electric charges move off an object is called **static discharge.**

Humidity If you rub a balloon on your clothing and then hold it next to a wall, it should stick. But the balloon may not always stick. Why is that? The answer could have to do with the weather.

EXPLORING Static Electricity

Static electricity involves the transfer of electrons from one object to another. Electrons are transferred by friction, conduction, or induction.

CHARGING BY FRICTION

When you rub two objects together, electrons move from one object to the other. This is known as charging by friction.

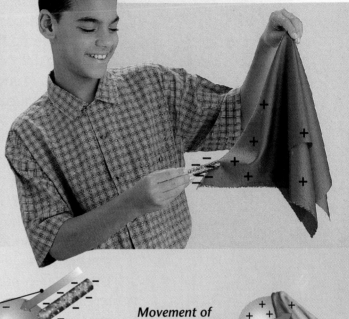

CHARGING BY CONDUCTION

When the charged rod or cloth touches the sphere, electrons are transferred by direct contact. This is known as conduction.

Movement of electrons

Becomes negatively charged

Movement of electrons

Becomes positively charged

CHARGING BY INDUCTION

During induction, charges within the spheres are rearranged without direct contact with the charged rod.

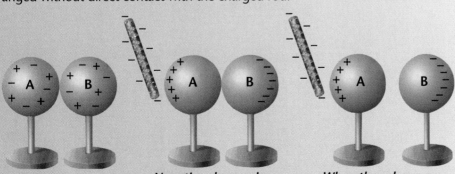

Neutral charge

Negative charges in the rod repel negative charges in the spheres.

When the spheres are separated, each one is charged.

Removing the charged rod leaves two charged spheres.

On a humid day, the air is filled with water molecules. Extra electrons on an object are carried off by molecules of water in the air. Thus the charges do not have a chance to build up on objects such as the balloon.

Sparks and Lightning Have you ever felt a shock from touching a doorknob after walking across a carpet? That shock is the result of static discharge. For example, as you walk across the carpet, electrons may rub off the soles of your shoes. This gives you a slight positive charge. When you touch the doorknob, electrons jump from the doorknob to your finger, making you neutral again.

Lightning is a dramatic example of static discharge. Lightning is basically a huge spark. During thunderstorms, air swirls violently. Water droplets within the clouds become electrically charged. Notice in Figure 5 that electrons collect in the lower parts of the cloud. To restore a neutral condition, electrons move from areas of negative charge to areas of positive charge. As electrons jump, they produce an intense spark. You see that spark as lightning.

Much of the lightning in a storm occurs between different regions of a cloud or between different clouds. But some lightning reaches Earth. This is because the cloud causes the surface of Earth to become charged by induction, as shown in Figure 5. Negative charges on the bottom of a cloud repel electrons, leaving the surface of Earth with a positive charge. If the charge buildup is sufficient, a huge spark of lightning is produced. The spark jumps between the cloud and Earth's surface or tall objects on the surface, such as trees or buildings.

Checkpoint **How can you get a shock from a doorknob?**

Figure 5 Lightning is a spectacular discharge of static electricity. Lightning can occur within a cloud, between two clouds, or between a cloud and Earth.

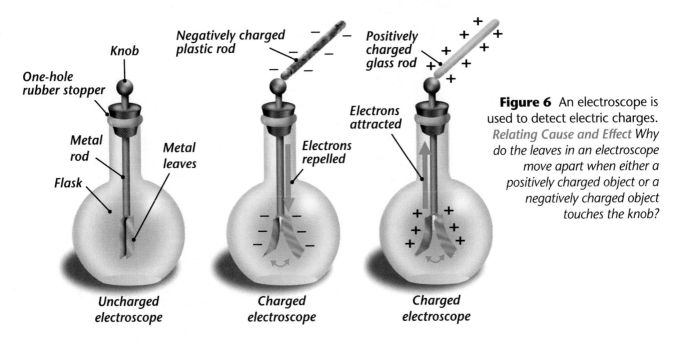

Figure 6 An electroscope is used to detect electric charges. *Relating Cause and Effect Why do the leaves in an electroscope move apart when either a positively charged object or a negatively charged object touches the knob?*

Labels (left to right):
- One-hole rubber stopper
- Knob
- Negatively charged plastic rod
- Positively charged glass rod
- Metal rod
- Metal leaves
- Flask
- Electrons repelled
- Electrons attracted
- Uncharged electroscope
- Charged electroscope
- Charged electroscope

Detecting Charge

Electric charge is invisible, but it can be detected by a special instrument called an **electroscope.** A typical electroscope consists of a metal rod with a knob at the top. At the bottom of the rod are two sheets, or leaves, of very thin metal (aluminum, silver, or gold). When the electroscope is uncharged, the leaves hang straight down.

When a charged object touches the metal knob, electric charge travels along the rod and into or out of the leaves. The leaves then have a net charge. Since the charge on both leaves is the same, the leaves repel each other and spread apart.

The leaves of an electroscope move apart in response to either negative charge or positive charge, so you cannot use an electroscope to determine the type of charge. You can use an electroscope only to detect the presence of charge.

Section 1 Review

1. How do particles with the same charge interact? How do particles with opposite charges interact?
2. What is static electricity?
3. What are the three ways by which static charge is produced?
4. How is static electricity discharged?
5. How does an electroscope detect charge?
6. **Thinking Critically Comparing and Contrasting** How are electric charges similar to magnetic poles? How are they different?

Science at Home

Rub a balloon against your hair and bring the balloon near one of your arms. Then bring your other arm near the front of a television screen that is turned on. Ask a family member to explain why the hairs on your arms are attracted to the balloon and to the screen. Explain that this is evidence that there is a static charge on both the balloon and the screen.

THE VERSORIUM

You are going to build a device that was first described in 1600 by Sir William Gilbert. He called this device a *versorium,* which is a Latin word meaning "turnabout." As you construct a versorium, you will use the skill of predicting.

Problem

Why does a versorium turn?

Materials

foam cup	plastic foam plate	pencil
aluminum foil	wool fabric	paper
scissors		

Procedure

1. Cut a piece of aluminum foil approximately 3 cm by 10 cm.
2. Make a tent out of the foil strip by gently folding it in half in both directions.
3. Push a pencil up through the bottom of an inverted cup. **CAUTION:** *Avoid pushing the sharpened pencil against your skin.* Balance the center point of the foil tent on the point of the pencil as shown.
4. Make a copy of the data table.
5. Predict what will happen if you bring a foam plate near the foil tent. Record your prediction in the data table.
6. Predict what will happen if you rub the foam plate with a piece of wool fabric and then bring it near the foil tent. Record your prediction.
7. Predict what will happen if you bring the rubbed wool near the foil tent. Again record your prediction.
8. Test each of your three predictions and record your observations in the data table.

DATA TABLE			
	Unrubbed Foam Plate	Rubbed Foam Plate	Rubbed Wool Fabric
Aluminum tent: Prediction			
Aluminum tent: Observation			
Paper tent: Prediction			
Paper tent: Observation			

9. What do you think would happen if you used a paper tent versorium instead of the aluminum foil? Record your prediction.
10. Test your prediction and record your observation.

Analyze and Conclude

1. At the beginning of the lab, is the foil negatively charged, positively charged, or neutral? Explain your answer.
2. What was the effect of rubbing the foam plate with the wool fabric?
3. Explain the behavior of the aluminum foil as the foam plate is brought near it. Explain the behavior as the wool fabric is brought near it.
4. After you bring the materials near it, is the foil negatively charged, positively charged, or neutral? Explain your answer.
5. Now think about the paper tent. How is it charged before and after you bring the objects near it? How do you know?
6. Explain the behavior of the paper versorium as the foam plate is brought near it, and as the wool fabric is brought near it.

7. Can you use a versorium to determine whether an object is positively or negatively charged? Explain.
8. Why should you avoid touching the foam plate or the wool fabric to your clothing or any other object while you are using it to test a versorium?
9. **Think About It** Did the aluminum foil and paper tent versoriums behave the way you predicted? What did you learn that could help you improve your predictions?

Design an Experiment

What other materials besides foam or wool might have an effect on the versorium? Think of other materials you could use to make the versorium tent. Make predictions, and test the materials to see if they respond in a fashion similar to the aluminum foil and paper tents.

2 Circuit Measurements

How Can Current Be Measured?

1. Obtain four pieces of wire with the insulation removed from both ends. Each piece should be about 25 cm long.

2. Wrap one of the wires four times around the compass as shown. You may use tape to keep the wire in place.

3. Build a circuit using the remaining wire, wrapped compass, two bulbs, and a D cell as shown. Adjust the compass so that the wire is directly over the compass needle.

4. Make sure the compass is level. If it is not, place it on a lump of modeling clay, so that the needle swings freely.

5. Observe the compass needle as you complete the circuit. Record the number of degrees the needle turns.

6. Repeat the activity using only one bulb, and again with no bulb. Record the number of degrees the needle turns.

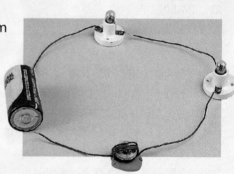

Think It Over

Inferring Based on your observations of the compass, when did the most current flow in your circuit? How can you explain your observations?

GUIDE FOR READING

◆ What causes electric current to flow?

◆ How does increasing voltage affect current?

◆ How does increasing resistance affect current?

Reading Tip Before you read, preview the boldfaced vocabulary terms. Write them down, leaving spaces between them for notes.

You're on a visit to a botanical garden. After a walk through the plush greenery, you rest by an artificial waterfall constructed in the middle of the garden. The continuous flow of water over the falls is soothing. You might be wondering what a waterfall could possibly have to do with electricity. Although there is an electric pump that keeps the water flowing, it is not the kind of pump that matters. The falling water itself, or any flowing liquid, is similar in some ways to the current in an electric circuit.

Electrical Potential

When water gets to the top of a waterfall it starts to fall down. When you lift something, you give it energy by doing work against the force of gravity. The type of energy that depends on position is called potential energy.

An object will move from a place of high potential energy to a place of low potential energy. The potential energy of the water is greater at the top of the waterfall than at the bottom. So water flows from the top to the bottom.

In a similar way, electrons in a circuit have potential energy. This potential energy, however, is related not to height but rather to the force exerted by electric fields. The potential energy per unit of electric charge is called **electrical potential.**

Voltage

Just as water flows downhill, electrons flow from places of higher potential to places of lower potential. The difference in electrical potential between two places is called the **potential difference.** It provides the force that pushes charge through a circuit. The unit of measure of potential difference is the volt (V). For this reason, potential difference is also called **voltage.** Electrons will flow as long as there is a potential difference, or voltage between two parts of a circuit.

Recall that the flow of electrons through a material is called electric current. Now you know what causes current to flow. **Voltage causes current to flow through an electric circuit.**

Figure 7 The diagram shows how a hidden pump feeds the waterfall in the photo. The movement of the water is similar to the current in an electric circuit.

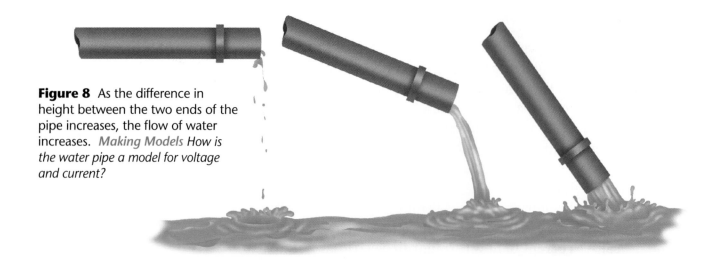

Figure 8 As the difference in height between the two ends of the pipe increases, the flow of water increases. *Making Models How is the water pipe a model for voltage and current?*

Voltage Sources

What happens to the water when it gets to the bottom of the waterfall in the botanical garden? If nothing brings the water back to the top, the water flow will quickly stop. But this waterfall has a pump that pushes the water back up to the top. Once the water returns to the top, it can flow back down again. Another way to describe this process is to say that the pump maintains the potential difference between the top and bottom of the falls. As long as this difference exists, the water can continue to flow.

An electric circuit also requires a device to maintain a potential difference, or voltage. A **voltage source** creates a potential difference in an electric circuit. Batteries and generators are examples of voltage sources.

You will learn more about voltage sources in the next chapter. For now, all you need to know is that a voltage source has two terminals. The potential difference, or voltage, between the terminals causes charges to move around the circuit.

Some voltage sources are stronger than others. You can compare voltage to the downward slant of the pipe near the top of the waterfall. If a pipe is nearly level, the water just trickles out as shown in Figure 8. But if one end is much higher than the other, the rate of water flow is greater. The greater the difference in height, the greater the flow of water. **Just as an increase in the difference in height causes a greater flow of water, an increase in voltage causes a greater flow of electric current.**

Resistance

The amount of water that flows through a pipe in the waterfall depends on more than just the angle of the pipe. It also depends on the pipe through which the water travels. A long pipe will resist

Figure 9 Water flows more easily through a short, wide pipe than through a long, narrow pipe. Similarly, electrons flow more easily through wires that are short and thick.

the flow of water more than a short pipe. And a thin pipe will resist the flow of water more than a wide pipe. In addition, a clogged pipe will offer more resistance than a clean pipe.

Current Depends on Resistance   In a similar way, the amount of current that flows in a circuit depends on more than just the voltage. Current also depends on the resistance offered by the material through which it travels. Recall that electrical resistance is the opposition to the flow of charge. **The greater the resistance, the less current there is for a given voltage.**

The resistance of a wire depends on the thickness and length of the wire. Long wires have more resistance than short wires. Thin wires have more resistance than thick wires. Resistance also depends on how well the material conducts current. Electrons are slowed down by interactions with atoms of the wire. Electrons flow freely through conductors, but not through insulators.

One more factor, temperature, affects electrical resistance. In Chapter 1 you learned that electrical resistance can decrease as temperature decreases. You can also say that as the temperature of most conductors increases, resistance increases as well.

Path of Least Resistance Perhaps you have heard it said that someone is taking the "path of least resistance." This means that the person is doing something the easiest way. In a similar way, if an electric current can travel through either of two paths, more of the current will travel through the path with lower resistance.

Have you ever seen a flock of birds perched comfortably on high-voltage power lines? The reason the birds don't get hurt is that current flows through the path of least resistance. Since a bird's body offers more resistance than the wire, current continues to flow directly through the wire without harming the bird.

✓ *Checkpoint* *What two factors affect the flow of a current?*

Down the Tubes

Use water to make a model of an electric current.

1. Set up a funnel, tubing, beaker, and ring stand as shown.

2. Have a partner start a stopwatch as you pour 200 mL of water into the funnel. Be careful not to let it overflow.

3. Stop the stopwatch when all of the water has flowed into the beaker.

Making Models How did your model represent electric current, voltage, and resistance?

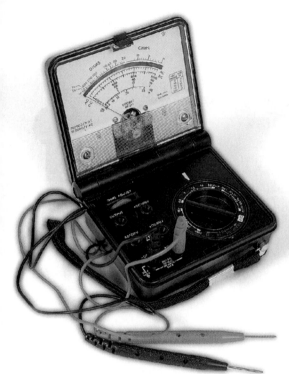

Figure 10 This multimeter can measure resistance, voltage, and small currents.

Ohm's Law

In the 1820s, the German physicist Georg Ohm experimented with many substances to study electrical resistance. He analyzed various types of wire in order to determine the characteristics that affect a wire's resistance. As a result of Ohm's valuable experiments, the unit of resistance is named the ohm (Ω).

How can you measure the resistance of a wire? In order to measure resistance, Ohm set up a voltage between two points on a conductor. He then measured the current produced. Potential difference, or voltage, is measured with a device called a **voltmeter.** Current, which has units of amps, is measured with a device called an **ammeter.** Voltmeters and ammeters are often combined into a single device like the one in Figure 10.

Ohm found that the resistance for most conductors does not depend on the voltage across them. A conductor or any other device that has a constant resistance regardless of the voltage is said to obey **Ohm's law.** Most of the conductors that you will learn about do obey Ohm's law.

Ohm's law states that the resistance is equal to the voltage divided by the current.

$$Resistance = \frac{Voltage}{Current} \quad \text{or} \quad Ohms = \frac{Volts}{Amps}$$

The letter R can be used to represent resistance, I to represent current, and V to represent voltage. This formula is shorter.

$$R = \frac{V}{I}$$

You can rearrange the resistance formula as follows.

$$I = \frac{V}{R} \quad \text{or} \quad V = IR$$

If any two of the values in these formulas are known, you can solve for the third value.

You can use the formulas to see how changes in resistance, voltage, and current are related. For example, what happens to current if voltage is doubled without changing the resistance? For a constant resistance, if voltage is doubled, current is doubled as well. Thus the greater the voltage, the greater the current.

What happens if, instead, you double the resistance without changing the voltage? If resistance is doubled, the current will be cut in half. So for a greater resistance, the current is less.

It is sometimes important to increase the resistance in a circuit in order to prevent too much current from flowing. Specially constructed resistors, some no larger than a grain of rice, are

Sample Problem

An automobile headlight is connected to a 12-volt battery. If the resulting current is 0.40 amps, what is the resistance of the headlight?

Analyze. You know the voltage and the current. You are looking for the resistance.

Write the formula. $R = \dfrac{V}{I}$

Substitute and solve. $R = \dfrac{12\ V}{0.40\ A} = 30\ \Omega$

Think about it. The answer makes sense because you are dividing the voltage by a decimal number. The answer should be greater than either number in the fraction, which it is.

Practice Problems

1. In a circuit, 0.5 A is flowing through the bulb. The voltage across the bulb is 4.0 V. What is the bulb's resistance?
2. In order for a waffle iron to operate efficiently, a current of 12 A must flow through its coils. If the resistance is 10 Ω, what must the voltage be?

added to circuits. Televisions, radios, and other similar devices contain dozens of such resistors.

Some resistors do not obey Ohm's law. For instance, the resistance of a light bulb increases when the bulb is turned on and the filament heats up. A filament has the lowest resistance before it heats up, and so a cold filament conducts the most current. That is one reason a bulb might burn out the instant you switch it on.

Section 2 Review

1. What is voltage?
2. How is voltage related to electric current?
3. How is resistance related to electric current?
4. **Thinking Critically** **Calculating** You light a light bulb with a 1.5-volt battery. If the bulb has a resistance of 10 ohms, how much current is flowing?
5. **Thinking Critically** **Relating Cause and Effect** In order to increase the amount of current flowing in a circuit, should you increase the voltage or the resistance? Explain.

Check Your Progress
CHAPTER PROJECT 2
Pick the event that will close your switch, for example, the closing of a door. To make your switch, you might tape one of the free wires to a door and the other wire to the frame of the door. The wires will touch when the door closes. Here are some other ideas to explore: an object falling, a slight vibration or breeze, or a container filling with salt water. Draw a circuit diagram that includes a battery, a switch, and a light bulb.

Real-World Lab

Constructing a
Dimmer Switch

Most light switches turn a light bulb on and off. There doesn't seem to be any setting in between. Suppose you wanted to find a way to dim lights slowly. Think about how you would design a switch that controls the brightness of a bulb.

Skills Focus

observing, predicting, designing experiments

Problem

What materials can be used to make a dimmer switch?

▲ **Engineer at a sound mixing board**

Materials

D cell   masking tape
flashlight bulb in a socket
thick lead from mechanical pencil
uninsulated copper wire, the same length as the
    pencil lead
rubber tubing, the same length as the pencil lead
1 wire 10–15 cm long
2 wires 20–30 cm long
2 alligator clips

Procedure

1. Construct the circuit shown in the photo. To begin, attach wires to the ends of the D cell.
2. Connect the other end of one of the wires to the bulb in a socket. Attach a wire with an alligator clip to the other side of the socket.
3. Attach an alligator clip to the other wire.
4. The pencil lead will serve as a resistor that can be varied—a variable resistor. Attach one alligator clip firmly to the tip of the pencil lead. Be sure the clip makes good contact with the lead. (*Note:* Pencil "lead" is actually graphite, a form of the element carbon.)
5. Predict how the brightness of the bulb will change as you slide the other alligator clip back and forth along the lead. Test your prediction.
6. What will happen to the brightness of the bulb if you replace the lead with a piece of uninsulated copper wire? Adapt your pencil-lead investigation to test the copper wire.

7. Predict what will happen to the brightness of the bulb if you replace the pencil lead with a piece of rubber tubing. Adapt your pencil-lead investigation to test the rubber tubing.

Analyze and Conclude

1. What variable did you manipulate by sliding the alligator clip along the pencil lead in Step 5?
2. What happened to the brightness of the bulb when you slid the alligator clip along the pencil lead?
3. Explain your reasoning in making predictions about the brightness of the bulb in Steps 6 and 7. Were your predictions supported by your observations?
4. Do you think that pencil lead has more or less resistance than copper? Do you think it has more or less resistance than rubber? Use your observations to explain your answers.

5. Which material tested in this lab would make the best dimmer switch? Explain your answer.
6. **Apply** If you wanted to sell your dimmer switch to the owner of a movie theater, how would you describe your device and explain how it works?

More to Explore

The volume controls on some car radios and television sets also contain variable resistors, called rheostats. The sliding volume controls on a sound mixing board are rheostats, as well. Homes and theaters may use rheostats to adjust lighting. Where else in your house would variable resistors be useful? (*Hint:* Look for applications where the output is graduated rather than all or nothing.)

DISCOVER

ACTIVITY

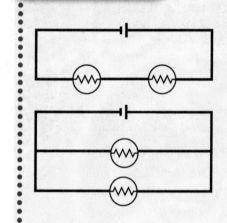

Do the Lights Keep Shining?

1. Construct both of the circuits shown using a battery, several insulated wires, and two light bulbs for each circuit.

2. Connect all wires and observe the light bulbs.

3. Now unscrew one bulb in each circuit. Observe the remaining bulbs.

Think It Over

Observing What happened to the remaining light bulbs when you unscrewed the first bulb? How can you account for your observations?

GUIDE FOR READING

◆ How many paths can current take in a series circuit?

◆ How does a parallel circuit differ from a series circuit?

Reading Tip As you read, create a table comparing series and parallel circuits.

It's a cool, clear night as you stroll by the harbor with your family. The night is dark, but the waterfront is bright thanks to the thousands of twinkling white lights that outline the tall ships. They make a striking view.

As you walk, you notice that a few of the lights are burned out. The rest of the lights, however, burn brightly. If one bulb is burned out, how can the rest of the lights continue to shine? The answer depends on how the electric circuit is designed. The parts of a circuit can be arranged in series or in parallel.

Figure 11 The lights that line the rigging of this ship are parts of a parallel circuit. If one goes out, the rest keep shining.

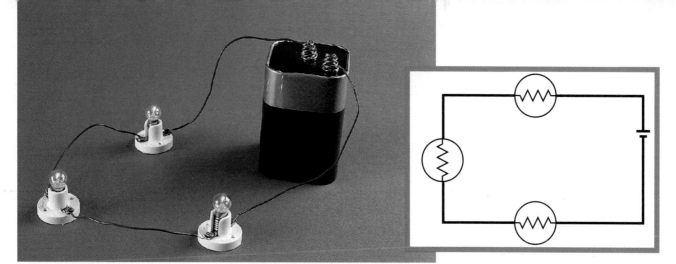

Figure 12 A series circuit provides only one path for the flow of electrons.
Applying Concepts What will happen to the other bulbs if one bulb burns out?

Series Circuits

If all the parts of an electric circuit are connected one after another, the circuit is a **series circuit.** Figure 12 illustrates a series circuit. **In a series circuit, there is only one path for the current to take.** For example, a switch and the device it controls are connected in series with each other.

One Path A series circuit is very simple to design and build, but it has some disadvantages. What happens if a bulb in a series circuit burns out? A burned-out bulb is a break in the circuit, and there is no other path for the current to take. So if one light goes out, all the lights go out.

Added Resistors Another disadvantage of a series circuit is that the light bulbs in the circuit become dimmer as more bulbs are added. Why does that happen? Think about what happens to the overall resistance of a series circuit as you add more bulbs. The resistance increases. Remember that if resistance increases, current decreases. So as light bulbs are added to a series circuit, the current decreases. The result is that the bulbs burn less brightly.

Ammeters Different meters are wired into circuits in different ways. Recall from the previous section that an ammeter is used to measure current. If you want to measure the current through some device in a circuit, the ammeter should be connected in series with the device.

☑ *Checkpoint* *How does resistance change as you add bulbs to a series circuit?*

Parallel Circuits

Could the lights on the ships have been connected in series? No—if the lights were part of a series circuit, all of the lights would have gone off when one burned out. What you saw, however, was that a few lights were burned out and the rest were brightly lit.

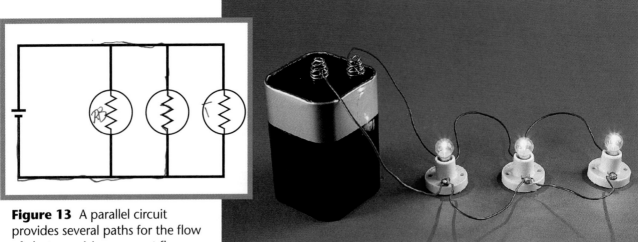

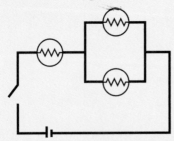

Figure 13 A parallel circuit provides several paths for the flow of electrons. More current flows, and the bulbs are brighter than in the series circuit.

The ships' lights were connected in parallel circuits. In a **parallel circuit,** the different parts of the circuit are on separate branches. Figure 13 shows a parallel circuit. **In a parallel circuit, there are several paths for current to take.** Notice that each bulb has its own path from one terminal of the battery to the other.

Several Paths What happens if a light burns out in a parallel circuit? If there is a break in one branch, current can still move through the other branches. So if one bulb goes out, the others remain lit. Switches can be placed along each branch so that individual bulbs can be turned on and off without affecting the others.

Added Branches What happens to the resistance of a parallel circuit when you add a branch? Although you might think that the overall resistance increases, it actually decreases. To understand this, consider the flow of water once again. Suppose water is being released from a reservoir held by a dam. If the water is allowed to flow through one pipe, a certain amount of water comes out. But if two pipes are used instead of one, twice as much water flows. The water will flow more easily because it has two paths to take. The same is true for a parallel circuit. As new paths, or branches, are added, the electric current has more paths to follow, and so total resistance decreases.

What does this tell you about current? If resistance decreases, the current must increase. The increased current travels along the new branch without affecting the original branches. So as you add branches to a parallel circuit, the brightness of the light bulbs does not change.

Voltmeters Recall from Section 2 that a voltmeter is used to measure voltage. When you measure the voltage across some device, the voltmeter and the device should be wired as parallel circuits.

Figure 14 Parallel circuits are used in your home.
Interpreting Diagrams How many circuits does this house have?

Household Circuits

Would you want the circuits in your home to be series circuits? Of course you would not. With a series circuit, all the electrical devices in your home would go off every time a light bulb burned out or a switch was turned off. Instead, the circuits in your home are parallel circuits.

Electricity is fed into a home by heavy wires called lines. These lines have very low resistance. You can see in Figure 14 that parallel branches extend out from the lines to wall sockets, appliances, and lights in each room. The voltage in these household circuits is 120 volts. Switches are located in places where they can be used to control one branch of the circuit at a time.

Section 3 Review

1. What are the two types of electric circuits? You can draw a diagram of each to explain your answer.
2. What happens to the bulbs in a series circuit if one of the bulbs burns out? Explain.
3. What happens to the bulbs in a parallel circuit if one of the bulbs burns out? Explain.
4. **Thinking Critically Comparing and Contrasting** You are building a string of lights using several bulbs. How is the brightness of the lights related to whether you connect the bulbs in series or in parallel?

Check Your Progress

CHAPTER PROJECT 2

Construct a circuit, either series or parallel, that lights a bulb when the switch is closed. Use the detector switch you designed earlier to close the circuit. Test the circuit to make sure that the switch closes when the event you are detecting occurs. Then make sure that the bulb lights when the switch is closed.

SECTION 4 Electrical Safety

DISCOVER

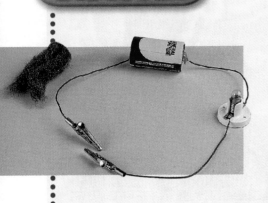

How Can You Blow a Fuse?

1. Begin by constructing the circuit shown using a D cell, a light bulb, and two alligator clips.

2. Pull a steel fiber out of a piece of steel wool. Wrap the ends of the steel fiber around the alligator clips.

3. Complete the circuit and observe the steel fiber and the bulb.

Think It Over

Developing Hypotheses Write a hypothesis to explain your observations.

GUIDE FOR READING

◆ How does a lightning rod protect a building?

◆ What safety devices are used in electric circuits?

◆ How is injury from an electric shock on the human body related to current?

Reading Tip As you read, make a list of ways that you can protect yourself from an electric shock.

The ice storm has ended, but it has left a great deal of destruction in its wake. Trees have been stripped of their branches, and a thick coating of ice covers the countryside. Perhaps the greatest danger is from the downed high-voltage lines left sparking in the streets. Residents are being warned to stay far away from them. What makes these power lines so dangerous?

Becoming Part of a Circuit

The sparks from those power lines should give you a clue as to what the danger is. One of the two parts of an electric company's circuit is a "live" wire carrying energy from the generating plant. The other part is a return or "ground" from the customer back to the generating plant. If a power line is damaged, the ground connection may be made through Earth itself. A person who touches a downed power line could create a short circuit to Earth through his or her body. A **short circuit** is a connection that allows current to take an unintended path. Rather than flowing through the return, or ground wire, the current would flow through the person.

The unintended path in a short circuit may offer less resistance than the intended path. So the current through a short circuit can be high. The result is a potentially fatal electric shock.

Exposed Wires Fallen high-voltage power lines are not the only potential source of electric shocks. Many people are hurt or killed by shocks from common household circuits. If you touch your hand to a 120-volt circuit, a potential difference, or voltage, is created between your hand and Earth. Since current flows when there is voltage, current will flow through your body.

Figure 15 Power must be shut off while work crews repair damaged lines.

The wires to the electrical devices in your home are protected by insulation. Sometimes that insulation wears off, leaving the wire exposed. If you touch such a wire, you become part of the circuit. You will get a painful, possibly harmful shock.

In some cases, the exposed wire is inside an electrical device such as a toaster. If the wire comes in contact with the outside metal case of the toaster, the entire toaster will conduct electricity. Then you could receive a shock from simply touching the toaster.

Resisting Current Is there any way to protect yourself if you become part of a circuit? The soles of your shoes will normally provide a large resistance between your feet and the surface of Earth. As a result, the current would not be enough to cause serious injury. But what happens if you're barefoot, or are standing in the bathtub when you touch the circuit? In either case, your resistance will be smaller. Ordinary tap water is not a very good conductor of electricity, but it does decrease your resistance. This means that the voltage can still produce enough current to seriously injure you.

Grounding

Additional grounding wires protect people from shocks. If a short circuit occurs in a device, current will go directly into Earth through a low-resistance grounding wire. In this way a person who touches the device will be protected.

Third Prong Have you ever noticed that some plugs have a third prong on them, as shown in Figure 16? The two flat prongs connect the appliance to the household circuit. This **third prong,** which is round, connects the metal shell of an appliance to the ground wire of a building.

In order to protect people from shocks, electrical systems are grounded. A circuit is electrically **grounded** when charges are able to flow directly from the circuit into the ground connection in the event of a short circuit.

Figure 16 The rounded prong on this plug is a safety device. *Relating Cause and Effect How does the third prong protect you if the appliance is faulty?*

Figure 17 A lightning rod attracts charges from a lightning bolt and carries them to Earth.

Lightning Rods With the idea of grounding, Benjamin Franklin was able to invent the lightning rod. A **lightning rod** is a metal rod mounted on the roof of a building in order to protect a building. Recall from Section 1 that charge is induced on Earth's surface during a thunderstorm. Lightning results from the transfer of charge from a charged cloud to an oppositely charged object on Earth. Franklin realized that charges are more crowded on pointed objects than on flat ones. So electrons in a lightning bolt are attracted to a pointed object such as a lightning rod.

A lightning rod is connected to a grounding wire. When lightning strikes the rod, charges flow through the rod, into the wire, and then into Earth. This protects the building.

If you think about how a lightning rod works, you will understand how to stay safe during a thunderstorm. It is not safe to stand under a tall conductor, such as a tall, wet tree. Even worse would be to hold a pointed metal object, such as an umbrella. If you are outside during a storm, the best way to protect yourself from lightning is to stay low and dry.

✓ *Checkpoint* *Why does lightning strike a lightning rod?*

Fuses and Circuit Breakers

A wire that carries more current than it is designed to carry will become hot. If it becomes too hot, it can melt the insulation on the wire. The hot wire can then come in contact with flammable materials in the walls of a building, causing a fire.

Electric current can become too high if a circuit is overloaded. Recall that as you add branches to a parallel circuit, the total resistance decreases and the current increases. If you use too many appliances at once, the current can become dangerously high. Overloading a circuit might result in a fire. **In order to prevent circuits from overheating, devices called fuses and circuit breakers are added to circuits.**

A **fuse** is a device that contains a thin strip of metal that will melt if too much current flows through it. When the strip of metal melts, or "blows," it breaks the circuit and stops the flow of current. If you have ever plugged in too many appliances at once, the electricity might have gone out because a fuse was blown. Once the overload is corrected, the fuse can be replaced and the electricity restored.

When a fuse burns out, it cannot be used again. To avoid the problem of having to replace fuses, circuits in new buildings are protected by devices called circuit breakers. A **circuit breaker** is a safety device that uses an electromagnet to shut off the circuit when the current gets too high. It's easy to reset the circuit breaker. All you have to do is pull back a switch—but only after turning off some of the appliances that are causing the high current in the circuit.

Electric Shocks

Why is it so important to protect the human body from electric shocks? The human body depends on electrical signals. Tiny electrical pulses, for example, control the beating of your heart. Similarly, electrical signals control your breathing and the movement of your muscles. If your body receives an electric current from a source outside it, the current will interfere with the normal processes within your body.

Current in the Body The shock you feel from static discharge after walking across a carpet on a dry day is not the same as the shock from touching a fallen power line. **The severity of an electric shock depends on the current.**

A current of less than 0.01 amp is almost unnoticeable. Between 0.1 amp and 0.2 amp, however, a current can be dangerous. Such a current might cause an irregular heartbeat and disrupt the flow of blood to your body. A current entering your hand can travel through your arm and across your heart. Currents greater than 0.2 amp cause burns and can stop your heart.

Resistance in the Body The current of an electric shock is related to voltage and resistance. The voltage is determined by the source of the shock. You can safely handle the 1.5-volt batteries for a radio, but you could be killed by touching power lines that carry thousands of volts.

The current that results from that voltage depends on the resistance of the human body. Resistance in the human body is affected by several factors. One factor is the conducting ability of body tissue. Living cells have a low resistance to electric current.

Figure 18 Both fuses and circuit breakers open a circuit when current gets too high.
Applying Concepts What is the maximum current that the yellow fuse can carry?

This is because the fluid in human cells contains ions, which are charged particles that conduct electricity.

Another factor is whether your skin is wet or dry. If your skin is very dry, your resistance might be very high. When your skin is wet, however, your resistance might be hundreds of times lower. So you are more likely to suffer a serious electric shock if you are wet than if you are exposed to the same voltage when you are dry.

Electrical Safety Tips

As you have learned, electricity is one of the most useful energy resources. But it can also be quite dangerous if not used carefully. Here are some important rules to remember when using electricity.

- Never handle electrical appliances when you or your hands are wet, or if you are standing in water.
- Never stick your fingers or any object other than a plug into an electrical outlet.
- Always unplug an electrical appliance before attempting to open or repair it.
- Never overload a circuit by attaching too many appliances to it.
- Never touch wires on power poles or wires that have fallen.
- Never use broken or frayed wires.

DANGER

HIGH VOLTAGE
AUTHORIZED PERSONNEL
ONLY

PELIGRO
ALTO VOLTAJE

Section 4 Review

1. Describe how a bolt of lightning passes through a lightning rod to the ground.
2. How are fuses and circuit breakers alike? How are they different?
3. Are all electrical shocks to the body equally dangerous? Explain.
4. **Thinking Critically** **Applying Concepts** Why do you think the Empire State Building in New York City is often hit by lightning?

Science at Home

Along with members of your family, find out if the circuits in your home are protected by fuses or circuit breakers. **CAUTION:** *Be careful not to touch the wiring as you inspect it.* How many circuits are there in your home? Make a diagram showing the outlets and appliances on each circuit. Explain the role of fuses and circuit breakers. Ask your family members if they are aware of these devices in other circuits, such as in a car.

SECTION 1 · Electric Charge and Static Electricity

Key Ideas

◆ Like charges repel each other and unlike charges attract each other.

◆ An electric field is produced in the region around an electric charge. The field can be represented by electric field lines.

◆ Static electricity results when electrons move from one object to another, or from one location to another within an object.

◆ During an electric discharge, charges leave a charged object, making the object neutral.

Key Terms

electric field
static electricity
friction
conduction

induction
conservation of charge
static discharge
electroscope

SECTION 2 · Circuit Measurements

Key Ideas

◆ Electric current flows when voltage is applied to a circuit.

◆ Voltage, which is measured in volts, is the potential difference between two places in a circuit.

◆ Resistance, which is measured in ohms, is the opposition to the flow of charge.

◆ If resistance is held constant, an increase in voltage produces an increase in current.

◆ If voltage is held constant, an increase in resistance produces a decrease in current.

Key Terms

electrical potential
potential difference
voltage
voltage source
voltmeter
ammeter
Ohm's law

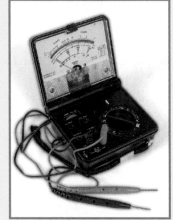

SECTION 3 · Series and Parallel Circuits

Key Ideas

◆ A series circuit is a circuit in which charges have only one path to flow through.

◆ A parallel circuit is a circuit that contains different branches through which charges can flow. Household circuits are parallel circuits.

Key Terms

series circuit   parallel circuit

SECTION 4 · Electrical Safety

INTEGRATING HEALTH

Key Ideas

◆ Fuses, circuit breakers, and grounded plugs are all important safety devices found in electric circuits.

◆ A lightning rod provides a conducting path to Earth, so that electric charges from lightning can travel directly into Earth without damaging a structure.

◆ The human body can be seriously injured by shocks, even those of less than one ampere.

Key Terms

short circuit	grounded	fuse
third prong	lightning rod	circuit breaker

Organizing Information

Venn Diagram Copy the Venn diagram comparing series and parallel circuits. Then complete it and add a title. (For more information on Venn Diagrams, see the Skills Handbook.)

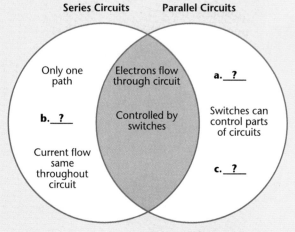

Series Circuits   Parallel Circuits

Only one path

Electrons flow through circuit

a. ?

b. ?

Controlled by switches

Switches can control parts of circuits

Current flow same throughout circuit

c. ?

Reviewing Content

 For more review of key concepts, see the Interactive Student Tutorial CD-ROM.

Multiple Choice

Choose the letter of the answer that best completes each statement.

1. A particle that carries a negative electric charge is called a(n)
   a. neutron.   **b.** atom.
   c. proton.   **d.** electron.
2. When you charge an electroscope by touching it with a charged balloon, the process is called
   a. friction.   **b.** conduction.
   c. induction.   **d.** grounding.
3. The potential difference that causes charges to move in a circuit is
   a. voltage.
   b. resistance.
   c. current.
   d. electric discharge.
4. An example of a voltage source is a
   a. voltmeter.   **b.** battery.
   c. resistance.   **d.** switch.
5. A circuit that is connected to Earth is said to be
   a. series.   **b.** parallel.
   c. grounded.   **d.** discharged.

True or False

If the statement is true, write true. If it is false, change the underlined word or words to make the statement true.

6. Your hair might be attracted to your comb as your hair and the comb become <u>oppositely</u> charged.
7. A neutral object becomes negatively charged when it <u>loses</u> electrons.
8. <u>Conduction</u> is the process of charging an object without touching it.
9. Electrical resistance is low in a good <u>conductor</u>.
10. A <u>circuit breaker</u> contains a thin strip of metal that melts if too much current passes through it.

Checking Concepts

11. Describe the electric field surrounding a charge.
12. What is static electricity?
13. What does it mean to say that an object is charged? Describe the three ways in which an object can become charged.
14. How is lightning related to static electricity?
15. State and describe Ohm's Law.
16. What units are used to measure voltage, current, and resistance?
17. What type of meter is used to measure current? To measure voltage? How should each meter be connected in a circuit?
18. Discuss three safety rules to follow while using electricity.
19. How do fuses and circuit breakers act as safety devices in a circuit?
20. **Writing to Learn** You are an electrician about to design the electrical wiring system for a new house. Your plans call for parallel circuits, but the owners insist that a series circuit will be simpler and cheaper. Write a letter, with diagrams, to the owners explaining why you need to use parallel circuits.

Thinking Critically

21. **Problem Solving** A toaster is plugged into a 120-volt socket. If it has a resistance of 20 ohms, how much current will flow through the toaster coils? Show your work.
22. **Classifying** Identify each of the following statements as characteristic of series circuits, parallel circuits, or both:
    a. $I = V \div R$
    b. Total resistance increases as more light bulbs are added.
    c. Total resistance decreases as more branches are added.
    d. Current in each part of the circuit is the same.
    e. A break in any part of the circuit will cause current to stop.
23. **Applying Concepts** Explain why the third prong of a grounded plug should not be removed.

Applying Skills

Use the illustration of an electric circuit to answer Questions 24–27.

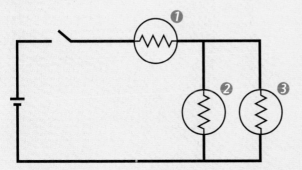

24. **Classifying** Is the circuit in the illustration series or parallel? Explain.
25. **Controlling Variables** Would the other bulbs continue to shine if you removed Bulb 1? Would they shine if you removed Bulb 2 instead? Explain your reasoning.
26. **Predicting** Will any of the bulbs be lit if you open the switch? Explain.

27. **Making Models** Redraw the circuit diagram to include a switch that controls only Bulb 3.

Performance CHAPTER PROJECT 2 Assessment

Project Wrap Up Prepare a description and circuit diagram for your display. If any parts of your alarm circuit are not visible, you should draw a second diagram showing how all the parts are assembled. Then present your alarm to your class and explain how it could be used.

Reflect and Record Describe the reliability of your switch. Does it work most of the time? All of the time? If your alarm circuit were to be used for a full year, would it still work? Draw sketches in your journal of parts of your alarm that would need to be redesigned so that it would last longer.

Test Preparation

Use these questions to prepare for standardized tests.

Use the diagram to answer Questions 28–30.

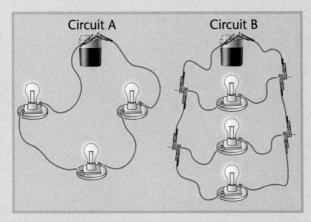

28. What will happen to the remaining bulbs in Circuit A if one of the bulbs burns out?
    a. They will continue to light, but they will be brighter.
    b. They will continue to light, but they will be dimmer.
    c. They will all go out.
    d. They will stay on until the current in the wire is used up and then go out.

29. Which of the following will happen if you add a fourth light to Circuit A?
    a. All of the lights will become brighter.
    b. The brightness of the lights will not change.
    c. The brightness of the lights located after the new light will become dimmer.
    d. All of the lights will become dimmer.

30. What will happen to the remaining bulbs in Circuit B if one of the bulbs burns out?
    a. They will remain lit with the same brightness.
    b. They will go out as well.
    c. They will continue to light, but they will be brighter.
    d. They will continue to light, but they will be dimmer.

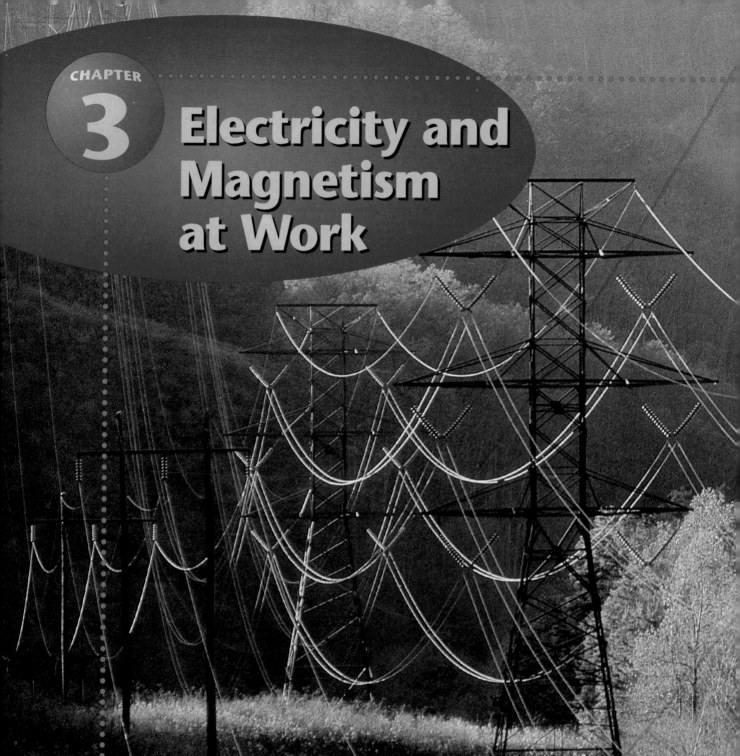

WEB ACTIVITY www.phschool.com

High-voltage transmission lines glisten in the sunlight.

PROJECT 3

Electrical Energy Audit

Have you ever heard someone complain about high electric bills? Electricity can be expensive, but there are good reasons why. Generating electricity and delivering it to customers is a complicated business.

In this chapter, you will discover how electricity is generated and used. As you work through the chapter, you will study electrical energy consumption in your home.

Your Goal To analyze the ways you use electricity at home and to determine how much electricity you and your family use.

To complete the project you will
◆ prepare a list of appliances in your home, including lights, that use electricity
◆ record the length of time each appliance is used during an average week
◆ calculate how much electrical energy is used to operate each appliance
◆ follow the safety guidelines in Appendix A

Get Started Begin by preparing a data table you can use to keep track of your observations. You should include columns for the name of the appliance, whether it is plugged in or battery operated, the primary use of the appliance, and the number of hours it is used each day.

Check Your Progress You'll be working on this project as you study this chapter. To keep your project on track, look for Check Your Progress boxes at the following points.

Section 1 Review, page 81: List all of the electric appliances in your home.

Section 2 Review, page 91: Calculate the amount of time each appliance is used during a week.

Section 3 Review, page 98: Calculate the amount of energy consumed by each appliance.

Wrap Up At the end of the chapter (page 109), you will calculate the total amount of electrical energy consumed and determine which appliance in your home uses the most electrical energy.

Integrating Chemistry 🔒

SECTION 4 **Batteries**

Discover Can You Make Electricity With Spare Change?
Skills Lab Electricity Grows on Trees

Electricity, Magnetism, and Motion

How Does a Magnet Move a Wire?

1. Make an electromagnet by winding insulated copper wire around a steel nail.

2. Make a pile of books, and place a ruler between the top two books.

3. Hang the electromagnet over the ruler so that it hangs free.

4. Complete the circuit by connecting the electromagnet to a switch and a battery.

5. Set a horseshoe magnet near the electromagnet. Then close the switch briefly and observe what happens to the electromagnet.

6. Reverse the wires connected to the battery and repeat Step 5.

Think It Over

Inferring What happened to the electromagnet when you closed the switch? Was anything different when you reversed the wires? How can you use electricity to produce motion?

GUIDE FOR READING

◆ How can electrical energy be converted into mechanical energy?

◆ What do galvanometers and electric motors do?

Reading Tip Preview the figures and captions. Then read to find out how magnetic forces and electric current are related to motion.

What comes to mind when you think about electricity? You may think of the bright lights of a big city, or the music from the radio in your bedroom. If you are familar with electric motors like the one in a movie projector, then you already know about a very important application of electricity. Electricity can produce motion.

Electrical and Mechanical Energy

As you have learned, magnets can produce motion. They can move together or move apart, depending on how their poles are arranged. You have also learned that an electric current in a wire produces a magnetic field similar to that of a magnet. So you can understand that a magnet can move a wire, as it would move another magnet.

The wire at the top of Figure 1 is placed in a magnetic field. When current flows through the wire, the magnetic force pushes the wire down. If the current is reversed, the magnetic force pulls the wire up. The direction in which the wire moves depends on the direction of the current.

The interaction between electricity and magnetism can cause something to move—in this case, a wire. The ability to move an object some distance is called **energy.** The energy associated with electric currents is called **electrical energy.** And the energy an object has due to its movement or position is called **mechanical energy.**

Energy can be changed from one form into another. **When a current-carrying wire is placed in a magnetic field, electrical energy is converted into mechanical energy.** This happens because the magnetic field of the current makes the wire move.

Checkpoint What is energy?

Galvanometers

The upper part of the wire in Figure 1 moves up or down in the magnetic field. What will happen if you place a loop in a magnetic field? Look at the rectangular loop of wire in Figure 2. The current in the wire travels up one side of the loop and down the other. In other words, current travels in opposite directions on the two sides of the loop.

Since the direction the wire moves depends on the direction of the current, the two sides move in opposite directions. Once each side has moved as far up or down as it can go, it will stop moving. The result is that the loop rotates half a turn.

The rotation of a loop of wire in a magnetic field is the basis of a device called a **galvanometer,** which is used to measure small currents. In a galvanometer several loops of wire are suspended between the poles of a magnet. The loops of wire are also attached to a pointer and to a spring, as in Figure 2. When current flows through the wire, the current produces a magnetic field. This field interacts with the field of the magnet, causing the loops of wire and the pointer to rotate. **Electric current is used to turn the pointer of a galvanometer.** The force of the

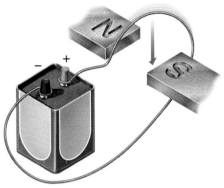

Force is down

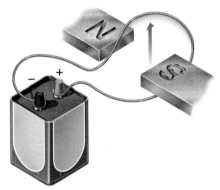

Force is up

Figure 1 The magnetic field of the permanent magnet interacts with the magnetic field produced by the current in the wire. *Interpreting Diagrams How does the direction of the current affect the force on the wire?*

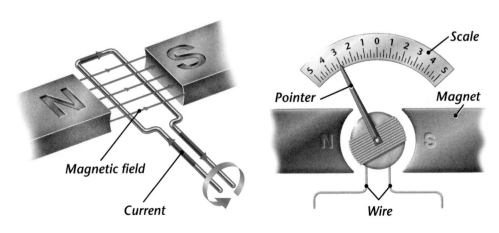

Scale

Pointer

Magnet

Magnetic field

Current

Wire

Figure 2 Since current travels in a different direction in each half of the wire loop (left), one side is pushed down while the other is pulled up. A galvanometer (right) uses loops of wire to move a pointer.

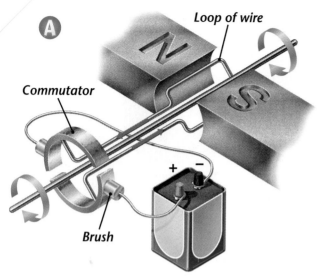

A

Loop of wire

Commutator

Brush

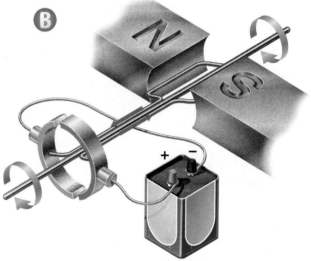

B

Figure 3 A loop of wire in a motor spins continuously. **A.** The magnetic field of the loop makes it rotate to a vertical position. **B.** As the loop of wire passes the vertical position, each half of the commutator makes contact with the opposite brush. The direction of current flow changes, and so does the direction of the magnetic force on the loop. The loop continues to spin in the same direction.

interaction of the fields acts against the spring. So the amount of rotation of the loops of wire and the pointer depends on the amount of current in the wire. A galvanometer has a scale that is marked to show how much the pointer turns for a known current. An unknown current can then be measured with a galvanometer.

☑ *Checkpoint* *How does a galvanometer work?*

Electric Motors

The wire in the magnetic field of a galvanometer cannot rotate more than half a turn. Suppose you could make a loop of wire rotate continuously. Instead of moving a pointer, the wire could turn a rod, or axle. The axle could then turn something else, such as the blades of a fan or blender. Such a device would be an electric motor. An **electric motor** is a device that uses an electric current to turn an axle.

An electric motor converts electrical energy into mechanical energy. An electric motor is different from a galvanometer because in a motor, a loop of current-carrying wire spins continuously.

How a Motor Works How can you make a loop of wire continue to spin? The direction of the force on the wire depends on the current and the magnetic field surrounding the coil. In a motor, current is reversed just as the loop gets to the vertical position.

This reverses the force on each side of the loop. The side of the loop that was pushed up on the left is now pushed down on the right. The side of the loop that was pushed down on the right is now pushed up on the left. The current reverses after each half turn so that the loop spins continuously in the same direction.

Parts of a Motor A **commutator** is a device that reverses the flow of current through an electric motor. You can see in Figure 3 that a commutator consists of two parts of a ring. Each half of the commutator is attached to one end of the loop of wire. When the loop of wire rotates, the commutator rotates as well. As it moves, the commutator slides past two contact points called **brushes**. Each half of the commutator is connected to the current source by one of the brushes.

As the loop of wire gets to the vertical position, each half of the commutator makes contact with the other brush. Since the current runs through the brushes, changing brushes reverses the direction of the current in the loop. Changing the direction of the current causes the loop of wire to spin continuously.

Instead of a single loop of wire, practical electric motors have dozens or hundreds of loops of wire wrapped around an iron core. This arrangement of wires and iron core is called an **armature**. Using many loops increases the strength of the motor and allows it to rotate more smoothly. Large electric motors also use electromagnets in place of permanent magnets.

Figure 4 This armature contains hundreds of coils of wire. *Interpreting Photos Where is the axle of the motor?*

Section 1 Review

1. How can electricity be used to produce motion?
2. What energy conversion takes place in an electric motor and a galvanometer?
3. What measurement can be made with a galvanometer?
4. Describe how the commutator and brushes of an electric motor operate.
5. **Thinking Critically Relating Cause and Effect** Why is it important to change the direction of the current in a motor?

Check Your Progress CHAPTER PROJECT 3
List the appliances in your home that use electricity. Check your home room by room. Throughout the course of one week, keep a record of the amount of time each appliance is used. Make a row in your data table for each appliance. Each row in the table will contain a space for the amount of time the appliance is used each day. You may want to leave a small note pad and pencil next to appliances used by others.

Building an Electric Motor

What does an electric trolley car have in common with a food blender, a computer disk drive, and a garage door opener? At first glance, these things may appear to be unrelated, but each one contains an electric motor. Electric motors are devices that convert electrical energy into motion. In this lab, you will build an operating electric motor.

Problem

How does an electric motor operate?

Skills Focus

making models, inferring

Materials

D cell
2 large paper clips
permanent disk magnet
3 balls of clay
empty film canister
pliers
sandpaper
2 insulated wires, approximately 15 cm each
enamel-coated wire, 22–24 gauge,
    approximately 1 meter

Procedure

1. Wrap about 1 meter of enamel-coated wire around a film canister. Leave approximately 5 cm free at each end.
2. Remove the film canister and wrap the two free ends three or four times around the wire coil to keep it from unwinding.
3. Use sandpaper to scrape off all the enamel from about 2 or 3 centimeters of one end of the coil of wire.

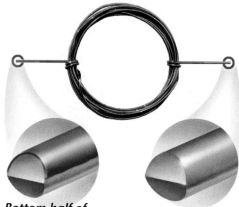

Bottom half of coating removed   *All coating removed*

4. Scrape off *half* of the enamel from about 2 or 3 centimeters of the other end of the wire. To do so, hold the coil edgewise and sand off the bottom half. See the illustration above.
5. Bend two paper clips as shown in the photo at the right. Hold them down with clay.
6. Place the free ends of the wire on the paper clips. Make sure the coil of wire is perfectly balanced. Adjust the paper clips and wire so that the coil can rotate freely.
7. Use clay to hold a permanent magnet in place directly below the coil of wire. The coil needs to be able to rotate without hitting the magnet.
8. Remove the insulation from the ends of two insulated wires. Use these wires to attach the paper clips to a D cell.
9. Give the coil a gentle push to start it turning. If it does not spin or stops spinning after a few seconds, check the following:
    ◆ Are the paper clips in good contact with the D cell?
    ◆ Will the coil spin in the opposite direction?
    ◆ Will the coil work on someone else's apparatus?

Analyze and Conclude

1. How is the flow of current through the coil related to how you sanded the ends of the enamel-coated wire in Steps 3 and 4?
2. A magnetic field is produced when the motor is connected to the D cell. Explain why.
3. Why does the coil of wire rotate?
4. What was the purpose of removing all the insulation from one end of the wire but only half from the other end?
5. Why did the coil have to be balanced in Step 6?
6. What factors did you find that affected the motion of the coil?
7. **Apply** Your motor is capable of producing motion, but it is not capable of doing much useful work. What are some ways you could modify your motor to make it capable of doing useful work?

Design an Experiment

You have demonstrated the principles of a simple electric motor. List three factors that may affect the motion of the coil. Design experiments to test these factors. What will happen to the motor if the connections to the voltage source are reversed? Try it and find out.

2 Generating Electric Current

DISCOVER
.... ACTIVITY....

Can You Produce Electric Current Without a Battery?

1. Obtain one meter of wire with the insulation removed from both ends.

2. Connect the wire to the terminals of a galvanometer or a sensitive multimeter.

3. Hold the wire between the poles of a strong horseshoe magnet. Observe the meter.

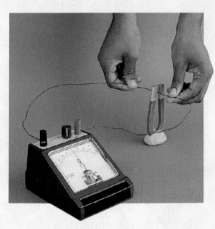

4. Move the wire up and down between the poles. Observe the meter.

5. Move the wire faster, and again observe the meter.

Think It Over
Developing Hypotheses In which steps does the meter indicate a current? Propose a hypothesis to explain how a current can exist without a battery. Be sure to use an "If . . . then . . ." statement.

GUIDE FOR READING

♦ What causes an electric current to be induced?

♦ How is a generator different from a motor?

♦ What are the main sources of energy for generating electricity?

Reading Tip Before you read, preview *Exploring Energy Resources* on pages 88 and 89. Write a list of any questions you have about generating electricity.

An electric motor operates because electricity produces motion. Is the reverse true—can motion produce electricity? In 1831, scientists found out that motion of a wire in a magnetic field can cause an electric current to flow. That discovery has allowed electricity to be supplied to homes, schools, and businesses all over the world.

Induction of Electric Current

Before you can understand how electricity is supplied by your electric company, you need to know how electricity is produced. Figure 5 shows part of a wire coil placed in a magnetic field. The coil of wire is connected to a galvanometer.

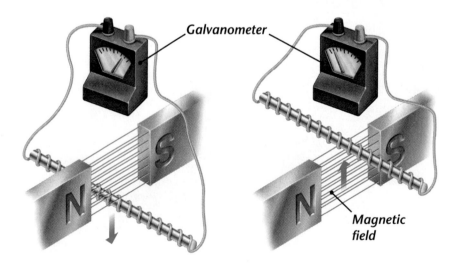

Figure 5 When a coil of wire is moved up or down in a magnetic field, a current is induced in the wire.

Galvanometer

Magnetic field

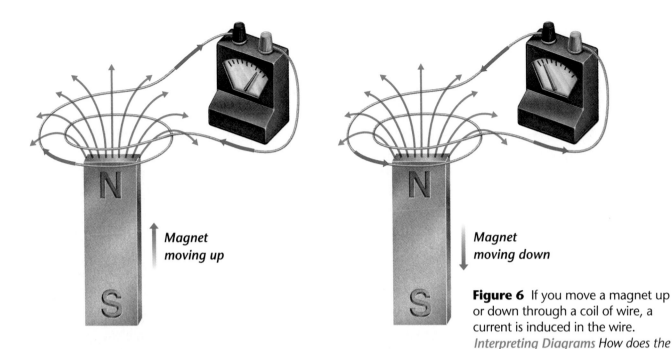

Magnet moving up

Magnet moving down

Figure 6 If you move a magnet up or down through a coil of wire, a current is induced in the wire.
Interpreting Diagrams How does the direction in which you move the magnet affect the current?

If the wire is held still, the galvanometer does not register any current. But if the wire is moved up or down, the galvanometer indicates an electric current flowing in the wire. The current is produced without a battery or other voltage source! You saw this for yourself if you did the Discover activity.

Figure 6 shows a similar experiment in which a magnet is moved instead of a wire. The result is the same as before. An electric current is produced in the wire.

The key to using a magnet to produce a current in a conductor, such as the wire, is motion. **An electric current will be produced in a conductor when the conductor moves across the lines of a magnetic field.** Either the conductor can move through the field of a magnet or the magnet itself can move. If the circuit is closed, a current flows in both cases.

Electromagnetic induction is the process of generating an electric current from the motion of a conductor through a magnetic field. The resulting current is an induced current.

Checkpoint What are the two ways that a wire and a magnet can produce an induced current?

Alternating and Direct Current

The direction of an induced current depends on the direction in which the wire or magnet moves. If, for example, the wire in Figure 5 is moved upward, the current travels in one direction. But if the wire is moved downward, the current travels in the opposite direction. **The flow of an induced current may be constant, or may change direction.**

Keeping Current

What factors affect an induced current? ACTIVITY

1. Obtain a wire about one meter long with the insulation removed from both ends.
2. Coil the wire into about 15 loops.
3. Connect the ends of the wire to a galvanometer or multimeter.
4. Move the end of a bar magnet halfway into the coil. Observe the meter.
5. One at a time, change the following and observe the galvanometer: the number of loops, the strength of the magnet, the direction of the magnet, and how far and how fast you move the magnet into the coil.

Interpreting Data Which variables affect your results the most? The least? Explain your observations.

What would happen if a wire in a magnetic field were moved up and down repeatedly? The induced current in the wire would reverse direction repeatedly as well. This kind of current is called **alternating current,** or AC. A current consisting of charges that move back and forth in a circuit is an alternating current. The electric current in the circuits in your home is alternating current.

A current consisting of charges that flow in one direction only is called **direct current,** or DC. A battery produces direct current. When a battery is placed in a circuit, electrons move away from one end of the battery, around the circuit, and into the other end of the battery.

Generators

An **electric generator** converts mechanical energy into electrical energy. An electric generator is the opposite of an electric motor. **An electric motor uses an electric current to produce motion. A generator uses motion to produce an electric current.**

AC Generators A simple AC generator is shown in Figure 7. As the axle is turned, the loop of wire rotates in the magnetic field. One side of the loop moves up, and the other side moves down. This motion induces a current in the wire. The current travels up one side of the loop and down the other.

After the loop turns halfway, each side of the loop reverses direction in the magnetic field. The side that moved up now moves down, and vice versa. As a result, the current in the wire changes direction as well. In this way the generator produces an alternating current.

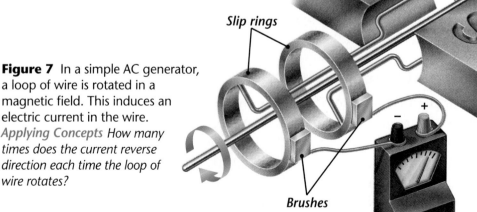

Figure 7 In a simple AC generator, a loop of wire is rotated in a magnetic field. This induces an electric current in the wire. *Applying Concepts How many times does the current reverse direction each time the loop of wire rotates?*

Slip rings

Brushes

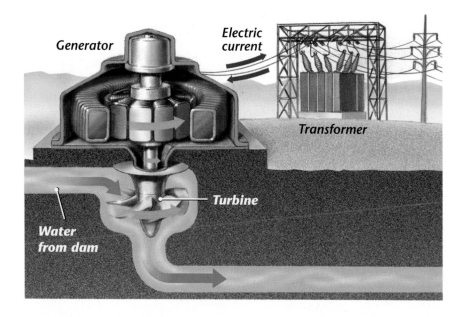

Figure 8 In most generators, a source of mechanical energy turns huge turbines such as this one. The turbine is attached to the armature of a generator, which then produces electric current.

How does the current travel to the rest of the circuit as the axle turns? **Slip rings** are attached to the ends of the wire loop in a generator. As the loop turns, the slip rings turn with it. The slip rings make contact with the brushes. The brushes are connected to the rest of the circuit, just as they are in an electric motor. The slip rings and brushes allow the loop to turn freely, yet still allow current to travel from the loop to the rest of the circuit. Large generators use armatures similar to those in a motor. They contain hundreds of loops of wire wrapped around an iron core.

DC Generators A DC generator is like an AC generator, except that it contains a commutator instead of slip rings. Replacing the slip rings in the generator in Figure 7 will make it look just like the DC motor in Section 1. In fact, a DC generator and a DC motor are the same thing. If you run electricity through a DC motor, it will spin. But if you spin the motor, you will produce electricity. The motor becomes a DC generator.

☑ *Checkpoint* *What is an electric generator?*

Turbines

A generator converts mechanical energy into electrical energy. When an electric company generates electricity, this mechanical energy usually involves huge turbines that turn. A **turbine** is a circular device made up of many blades. The turbine shown in Figure 8 is just like a propeller turned by water.

Not all turbines are turned by water. **Flowing water from a dam, wind, steam from the burning of fuels, and even the ocean's tides can be used to turn turbines.** Several sources of energy are shown in *Exploring Energy Resources* on the next two pages.

Classifying

1. Connect the wires from two hand generators to each other.
2. Have a partner hold one generator as you turn the crank on the other.
3. Now hold your generator as your partner turns the crank on the other one. Do not crank both generators at the same time.

Which hand generator acts like a motor and which acts like a generator? How do you know?

EXPLORING Energy Resources

Electric power can be produced in several ways. Each kind of generating plant converts a particular kind of energy into electrical energy.

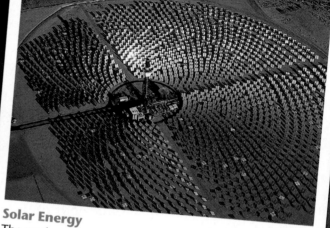

Solar Energy
The sun's rays can be focused on a tower by large mirrors to boil water. The resulting steam then turns a turbine. One type of solar cell can also collect the sun's energy and convert it directly into electrical energy.

Nuclear Energy
A tremendous amount of energy is stored in the nucleus of an atom. When the nucleus is split, the energy that is released is used to heat water. The water turns into steam, which expands and turns a turbine.

Energy From Falling Water
Hydroelectric plants near the bases of dams or waterfalls use water to turn turbines.

Geothermal Energy
In a few locations on Earth, underground water heated by molten rock turns to steam. This steam, which can be obtained through steam vents or drilling, is then used to turn a turbine.

Energy From Fossil Fuels
Coal, natural gas, and oil can be burned in generating plants to produce steam. The steam pushes against the blades of a turbine, causing it to turn.

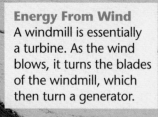

Energy From Wind
A windmill is essentially a turbine. As the wind blows, it turns the blades of the windmill, which then turn a generator.

Tidal Energy
As tides move in and out in a basin behind a dam, the moving water can be used to turn a turbine.

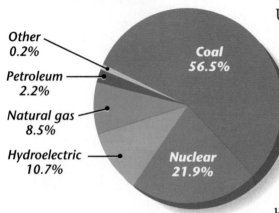

Figure 9 This circle graph shows which energy resources are used most commonly to generate electricity in the United States.

Coal
56.5%

Nuclear
21.9%

Other
0.2%

Petroleum
2.2%

Natural gas
8.5%

Hydroelectric
10.7%

Generating Electricity

The leading resources for generating electricity in the United States are shown in the graph in Figure 9. Energy resources are limited by their availability on Earth. So not all energy resources are used as readily as others. Some resources have very small roles in generating electricity. Unless you live in certain parts of the United States, you may never have seen an array of windmills, solar mirrors, or even a dam. One thing to remember about the graph is that it shows only resources used to generate electricity. The gasoline that is burned in cars, and the natural gas that heats houses, are not shown here.

Cost is a very important factor in the generation of electricity. But the cost in dollars and cents is not the only thing to consider. Figure 10 summarizes some of the major positive and negative features of these energy resources.

Figure 10 No energy resource is ideal. All have positive and negative features.
Interpreting Tables What are the cons of hydroelectric energy?

Pros and Cons of Energy Resources		
Resource	**Pros**	**Cons**
Coal	Moderate cost, large supply	Large deposits are localized. Mining damages land and water and is hazardous to miners. Burning coal produces air pollution.
Oil	Moderate cost, adequate supply	Large deposits are localized, and prices are variable. Oil spills damage land and water.
Natural gas	Moderate cost, adequate supply	Large deposits are localized.
Nuclear power	No air pollution	Construction of reactors is expensive. Waste disposal is an unsolved problem. There is a threat of nuclear accidents.
Hydroelectricity	Low cost, no wastes	Unused sites for dams are rare. Dams flood large areas and disturb wildlife in rivers.
Wind	Moderate cost, no wastes, inexhaustible supply	Winds are variable. Wind farms require large areas of land.
Sun	No wastes, inexhaustible supply	Solar generating plants are expensive. Sunlight varies with weather and time of day. Generating plants require large areas of land.
Geothermal power	Moderate cost, low operating costs	Geothermal sites are uncommon. Air pollution may be produced along with steam.
Tides	No wastes	Tidal sites are very uncommon. Power varies with tides. Construction is expensive.

One factor that does not appear in the table is carbon dioxide. Burning any fossil fuel releases carbon dioxide into the atmosphere. Scientists believe that the release of carbon dioxide may cause climates all over the world to become warmer. This climate change is called global warming. Reducing the use of fossil fuels would reduce the risk of climate change.

INTEGRATING ENVIRONMENTAL SCIENCE Some sources of energy in Figure 10 are said to be renewable. A **renewable resource** is one that can be replaced in nature at a rate close to the rate at which it is used. In other words, the supply of a renewable resource is not fixed. Water is a renewable resource because the water supply is continually replaced by rain. Wind energy, tidal energy, geothermal energy, and solar energy are renewable resources as well.

Other sources of energy are said to be nonrenewable. A **nonrenewable resource** is one that exists in a fixed amount. The supply of a nonrenewable resource is limited. The supply cannot be replaced once it is used up. Fossil fuels, such as coal, oil, and natural gas, are nonrenewable resources. As you can see in Figure 9, coal leads all other sources in importance.

It is unlikely that the world's nonrenewable energy supplies will run out in your lifetime. Deposits of coal, in particular, are quite large. The United States has about one fifth of the world's coal. But fossil fuels cannot be replaced. Eventually even the largest deposits will be used up. For this reason, and to reduce the risk of global warming, the world's energy sources will probably shift away from fossil fuels.

Figure 11 A house like this one does not need to be connected to an electrical generating plant. Solar cells produce all of its electricity.

Section 2 Review

1. What is induction of electric current?
2. Compare and contrast a motor and a generator.
3. How is alternating current different from direct current?
4. Describe the different ways of spinning turbines to generate electricity.
5. **Thinking Critically Comparing and Contrasting** What is the difference between a renewable and a nonrenewable energy source? Give an example of each.

Check Your Progress **CHAPTER PROJECT 3**
After one week, add the numbers in the row indicating the daily use for each appliance. This will tell you the number of hours the appliance was used in a week. (*Hint:* Convert minutes to decimal portions of hours. For example, 6 minutes = 0.1 hour.)

SECTION
③ Using Electric Power

DISCOVER • ACTIVITY

How Can You Make a Bulb Burn More Brightly?

1. Attach a light bulb in its socket to a hand generator as shown.
2. Slowly crank the generator. Observe the brightness of the bulb.
3. Crank the generator a little faster and again observe the bulb.
4. Crank the generator quickly and observe the bulb once more.

Think It Over
Posing Questions How does the speed at which you crank the generator affect the brightness of the bulb? What questions do you need to ask to explain how the rate of generating electrical energy is related to the brightness of the bulb?

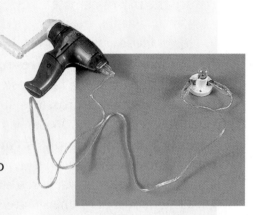

GUIDE FOR READING

◆ How can you calculate power and energy use?
◆ What is the function of a transformer?
◆ What makes alternating current suitable for long-distance transmission of energy?

Reading Tip As you read, use the headings in the section as an outline. Take notes in order to add details to your outline.

When you turn on an electrical appliance such as a toaster, stove, or microwave oven, you are using electrical energy. Each of these appliances converts electrical energy into heat. You can feel the heat given off as the appliance and its contents warm up. When you want heat, you usually want to convert a large amount of electrical energy in a short time. This is the same as saying you want a high rate of energy conversion.

Figure 12 Arc welding produces a white-hot glow as electrical energy is converted into heat.

Electric Power

The rate at which energy is converted from one form into another is known as **power.** The unit of power is the watt (W), named for inventor James Watt. Watt made important improvements to the steam engine in the 1700s.

Power Ratings You are already familiar with different amounts of electric power. The power rating of a bright light bulb, for example, might be 100 W. The power rating of a dimmer bulb might be 60 W. The bright light bulb converts (or uses) electrical energy at a faster rate than a dimmer bulb.

Calculating Power The power used by a bulb or appliance depends on two factors: voltage and current. **You can calculate power by multiplying voltage by current.**

$$Power = Voltage \times Current$$

or

$$Watts = Volts \times Amps$$

Using the symbols P for power, V for voltage, and I for current, this equation can be rewritten.

$$P = V \times I$$

You can rearrange this equation to solve for current.

$$I = \frac{P}{V}$$

Current is equal to power divided by voltage. As long as you have any two of the values in the equation, you can solve for the third.

Power Ratings for Common Appliances

Appliance	Power (W)
Stove	6,000
Clothes dryer	5,400
Water heater	4,500
Washing machine	1,200
Dishwasher	1,200
Hair dryer	1,200
Iron	1,100
Microwave oven	1,000
Coffee maker	1,000
Toaster	850
Food processor	500
Fan	240
Color television	100
Clock radio	12

Figure 13 Electrical appliances use energy at different rates. *Applying Concepts How many microwave ovens use the same amount of power as one stove?*

Sample Problem

A household light bulb has approximately 0.5 amps of current flowing through it. Since the standard household voltage is 120 volts, what is the power rating for this bulb?

Analyze. You know the current and the voltage. You need to find the power.

Write the formula. $P = V \times I$

Substitute and solve. $P = V \times I = 120 \text{ volts} \times 0.5 \text{ amps} = 60 \text{ watts}$

Think about it. The answer is reasonable, because 60 watts is a common rating for household light bulbs.

Practice Problems

1. A flashlight bulb uses two 1.5-volt batteries in series to create a current of 0.5 amps. What is the power rating of the bulb?
2. A hair dryer has a power rating of 1,200 watts and uses a standard voltage of 120 volts. What is the current through the hair dryer?

Paying for Energy

The electric bill that comes to your home charges for energy use, not power. Energy use depends on both power and time. Different appliances convert electrical energy at different rates. And you use some appliances more than others. **The total amount of energy used by an appliance is equal to the power consumption multiplied by the time the appliance is in use.**

$$Energy = Power \times Time$$

$$E = P \times T$$

Electric power is usually measured in thousands of watts, or kilowatts (kW). And time is measured in hours. So the unit of electrical energy is the kilowatt-hour (kWh).

$$Kilowatt\text{-}hours = Kilowatts \times Hours$$

Ten 100-watt light bulbs turned on for one hour use 1,000 watt-hours, or 1 kilowatt-hour, of energy.

The electrical energy that flows into your home is measured by a meter. As more lights and appliances are turned on, you can observe the meter turning more rapidly. The electric company uses the meter to keep track of the number of kilowatt-hours used. You pay a few cents for each kilowatt-hour.

Transformers

Generating electricity costs money, and so your electric company is very interested in efficient ways of transmitting current. The most efficient way to transmit current over long distances is to maintain very high voltages—from about 11,000 volts to 765,000 volts. But electricity is used at much lower voltages (about 120 volts in the United States). How is this problem solved?

Voltage must be increased before it is sent out over the wires from a generating plant. Then it must be reduced again before it is distributed to customers. **A device that increases or decreases voltage is called a transformer.** A **transformer** consists of two separate coils of insulated wire wrapped around an iron core. One coil, called the primary coil, is connected to a circuit in which an alternating current flows. The other coil, the secondary coil, is connected to a separate circuit that does not contain a voltage source.

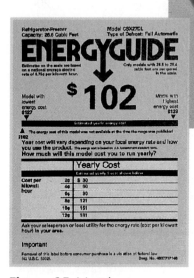

Figure 14 The total electrical energy consumption for your home can be read from a meter like this one.

Figure 15 Most large electrical appliances have labels showing the amount of energy they consume in a year. A typical refrigerator uses more than 700 kWh per year, or about 2 kWh per day.

When a current flows in the primary coil, it produces a magnetic field. The magnetic field changes as the current alternates. This changing magnetic field is like a moving magnetic field. It induces a current in the secondary coil.

Can a transformer work with direct current? The answer is no. A transformer works only if the current in the primary coil is changing. If the current does not change, the magnetic field does not change. No current will be induced in the secondary coil.

☑ *Checkpoint* *What are the parts of a transformer?*

Changing Voltage

How does a transformer change voltage? The answer has to do with the number of loops in the coils. If the number of loops in the primary and secondary coils are the same, the induced voltage is the same as the original voltage. However, if there are more loops in the secondary coil than in the primary coil, the voltage in the secondary coil will be greater. A transformer that increases voltage is called a **step-up transformer.**

Suppose there are fewer loops in the secondary coil than in the primary coil. The voltage in the secondary coil will be less than in the primary coil. A transformer that decreases voltage is called a **step-down transformer.**

Step-down Transformer

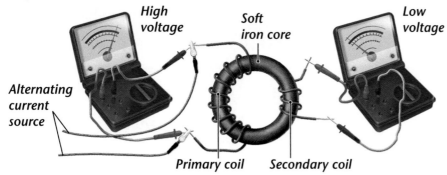

Step-up Transformer

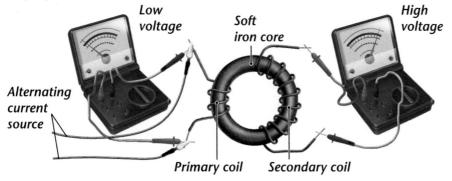

Figure 16 A step-up transformer increases voltage. A step-down transformer decreases voltage. *Comparing and Contrasting Compare the two transformers. Which transformer has a greater number of loops in the primary coil? In the secondary coil?*

Some electrical devices contain tranformers of their own. For example, fluorescent lights, televisions, and X-ray machines require higher voltages than house current. So they contain step-up transformers. Other devices such as doorbells, electronic games, and answering machines, require lower voltages. They contain step-down transformers.

The War of the Currents

Modern electric companies use alternating current and transformers to distribute electric power. But about 100 years ago, there was a great deal of controversy over AC and DC.

SCIENCE & History

The History of Electric Power

Several scientists were responsible for bringing electricity from the laboratory into everyday use.

1820
Electromagnetism

Hans Christian Oersted discovers that an electric current creates a magnetic field. The relationship between electricity and magnetism is called electromagnetism.

1800	1820	1840

1830–1831
Electric Induction

Michael Faraday and Joseph Henry each discover that an electric current can be induced by a changing magnetic field. Understanding induction makes possible the development of motors and generators.

Thomas Edison set up one of the first electric companies, the Edison Electric Light Company, in New York City. It supplied direct current at about 120 volts. Current traveling through long wires at that voltage would lose much of its energy in warming the wires. So Edison expected power generating plants to be small and quite close together.

A young immigrant from Croatia, Nikola Tesla, worked for Edison as an engineer for a short time. Tesla felt strongly that distribution of electricity to homes could be done safely and far more efficiently using alternating current. Generating plants could be located far apart. Step-up and step-down transformers

In Your Journal

Find out more about the work of Michael Faraday, Joseph Henry, or Hans Christian Oersted. Write a letter to a friend in which you describe your work as a research assistant for the scientist you choose. Include descriptions of his experimental procedures and the equipment he uses. Tell how his work has led to surprising discoveries.

1893

World's Columbian Exposition

Nikola Tesla's system of alternating current is used to light the world's fair in Chicago.

1860　　　　　1880　　　　　1900

1882

Direct Current

Thomas Edison opens his generating plant in New York City. The Pearl Street Station consists of six DC generators, serving an area of about 2.6 square kilometers.

1888

Alternating Current

Nikola Tesla receives patents for a system of distributing alternating current.

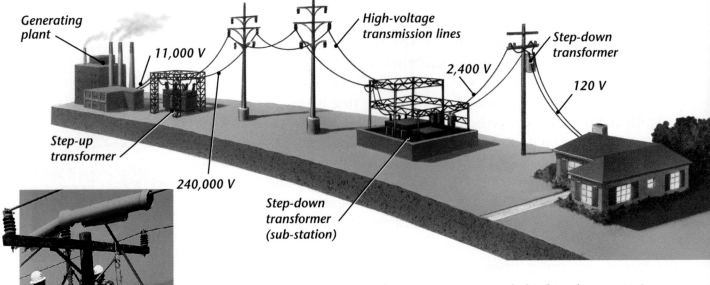

Generating plant

11,000 V

High-voltage transmission lines

Step-down transformer

Step-up transformer

240,000 V

2,400 V

120 V

Step-down transformer (sub-station)

Figure 17 Voltage is increased and decreased as alternating current is transmitted from its source to your home. This photo shows a transformer like the ones you might see in your neighborhood.

then would allow safe transmission with high voltages. **Using alternating current with transformers would reduce energy losses in the long transmission wires.** Tesla invented, among other devices, the first alternating current motor.

Edison thought that high voltages were dangerous. He also wanted to protect his investments in DC generating equipment.

For about 15 years, disagreement raged over which form of current was best. Tesla and the industrialist George Westinghouse eventually won the battle. In 1893 Tesla and Westinghouse were invited to light the World's Columbian Exposition in Chicago using alternating current. The lighting was spectacular! Tesla and Westinghouse were then given a contract for an alternating current system to harness the energy of Niagara Falls. Alternating current was so successful that eventually Edison's own company converted to alternating current as well. Alternating current has been used ever since.

Section 3 Review

1. What is electric power and how is it calculated?
2. How do electric companies calculate electrical energy?
3. How does a transformer work?
4. Explain why transformers are used in the transmission of electricity.
5. **Thinking Critically Problem Solving** One jelly-filled donut contains an amount of energy equal to about 0.5 kilowatt-hours. If that energy could be converted into electrical energy, how long would it keep a 15-watt night light lit?

Check Your Progress CHAPTER PROJECT 3
Determine the power ratings, in kilowatts, of the devices you listed. If power is not indicated on the device, you can calculate it from current and voltage. Find the amount of energy used by multiplying the power by the number of hours the device was used in a week. **CAUTION:** Get permission and adult help before looking for this information, especially on large appliances.

SECTION 4 Batteries

DISCOVER •• ACTIVITY

Can You Make Electricity With Spare Change?

1. Clean a penny with vinegar. Wash your hands.

2. Cut a 2-cm × 2-cm square from a paper towel and a similar square from aluminum foil.

3. Stir salt into a glass of warm water until the salt begins to sink to the bottom. Then soak the paper square in the salt water.

4. Put the penny on your desktop. Place the wet paper square on top of it. Then place the piece of aluminum foil on top of the paper.

5. Set a voltmeter to read DC volts. Touch the red lead to the penny and the black lead to the foil. Observe the reading on the voltmeter.

Think It Over

Observing What happened to the voltmeter? What type of device did you construct?

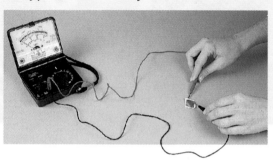

Electric generators are excellent sources of electrical energy. But what do you do if you need electrical energy on the go? Researchers have put a tracking device on the moose in Figure 18. The moose will carry the device deep into the wilderness. Fortunately, the tracking device contains a battery. Batteries are useful in many devices, such as portable radios, flashlights, toys, and calculators, to name just a few. In this section, you'll find out how a battery produces electrical energy.

GUIDE FOR READING

◆ How can chemical reactions generate electricity?

◆ How does a battery differ from an electrochemical cell?

Reading Tip As you read, write a phrase or sentence defining each boldfaced term, using your own words.

Figure 18 A battery-powered transmitter will allow researchers to study the movements of this brown-eyed, handsome moose.

The First Battery

A generator converts energy from one form into another, and so does a battery. Instead of mechanical energy, however, batteries start with chemical energy. **Chemical energy** is energy stored in chemical compounds.

Luigi Galvani The research that led to the development of the battery came about by accident. In the late 1700s, an Italian physician named Luigi Galvani was studying the anatomy of a frog. He was using a brass hook to hold a leg muscle in place. As he touched the hook to an iron railing, he noticed that the leg twitched. Galvani hypothesized that there was some kind of "animal electricity" present only in living tissue. This hypothesis was later proven to be incorrect.

Alessandro Volta An Italian scientist named Alessandro Volta argued that the electrical effect Galvani observed was actually a result of a chemical reaction. A **chemical reaction** is a process in which substances change into new substances with different properties. In this case, Volta believed that a chemical reaction occurred between the two different metals (the iron railing and the brass hook) and the salty fluids in the frog's leg muscle.

To prove his hypothesis, Volta placed a piece of silver on top of a piece of zinc. On top of the silver he added a piece of paper that had been soaked in salt water. Then he repeated the layers: zinc, silver, paper, zinc, and so on. Volta found that if he connected wires to the metals, current flowed. When he added more layers, more current flowed. If you did the Discover activity, you constructed a stack similar to Volta's.

Figure 19 Alessandro Volta stacked metal plates and paper, making the first battery. Volta is shown demonstrating his battery to Napoleon in 1801.

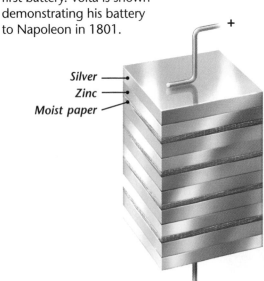

Silver
Zinc
Moist paper

+

−

Volta had designed and built the first electric battery. In the year 1800, Volta made his discovery public. Although his battery was much weaker than those made today, it produced a current for a relatively long period of time. It was the basis of more powerful modern batteries.

☑ *Checkpoint* *What metals were used in Volta's experiments on electricity?*

Electrochemical Cells

In Volta's setup, each pair of metal pieces separated by paper soaked in salt water acted as an electrochemical cell. An **electrochemical cell** is a device that converts chemical energy into electrical energy. An electrochemical cell consists of two different metals called **electrodes.** The electrodes are partially immersed in a substance called an electrolyte. An **electrolyte** is a substance that conducts electric current. Volta used silver and zinc as electrodes and salt solution as his electrolyte.

A Simple Cell Look at the electrochemical cell in Figure 20. In this particular cell, the electrolyte is dilute sulfuric acid. Dilute means that the sulfuric acid has been mixed with water.

One of the electrodes in this cell is made of copper and the other is made of zinc. The part of an electrode above the surface of the electrolyte is called a **terminal.** The terminals are used to connect the cell to a circuit.

Chemical reactions occur between the electrolyte and the electrodes in an electrochemical cell. These reactions cause one electrode to become negatively charged and the other electrode to become positively charged. In this case, the zinc electrode becomes negatively charged and the copper electrode becomes positively charged. Because the electrodes have opposite charges, there is a voltage between them. Recall that voltage causes charges to flow. If the terminals are connected by a wire, electrons will flow from one terminal to the other. In other words, the electrochemical cell produces an electric current in the wire. Charges flow back through the electrolyte to make a complete circuit.

How do you know which metal will become the positive terminal and which will become the negative terminal? The answer depends on the metal strips used. Some metals, such as zinc and aluminum, are more likely to release electrons into the wire than other metals, such as copper and silver.

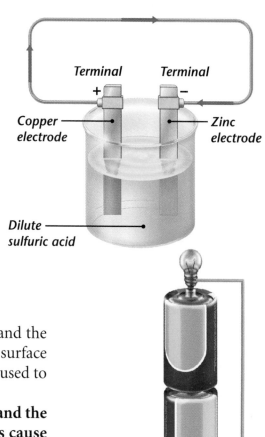

Figure 20 An electrochemical cell consists of two electrodes made of different metals, and an electrolyte. *Predicting What would you expect the voltage to be if you connected two cells together as in a flashlight?*

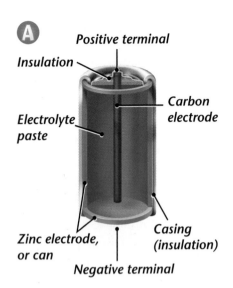

A

Positive terminal

Insulation

Electrolyte paste

Carbon electrode

Zinc electrode, or can

Casing (insulation)

Negative terminal

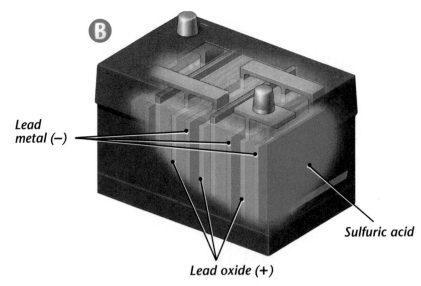

B

Lead metal (−)

Sulfuric acid

Lead oxide (+)

Figure 21 Electrochemical cells can be dry or wet. **A.** This diagram shows the parts of a typical dry cell. The electrolyte of a dry cell is a paste. **B.** A car battery is made up of several wet cells. A wet cell uses a liquid electrolyte.

Combining Electrochemical Cells Several electrochemical cells can be stacked together to form a battery. A **battery** is a combination of two or more electrochemical cells in a series. Today, single cells are often referred to as batteries. So the "batteries" you use in your flashlight are technically cells rather than batteries.

In a battery, two or more electrochemical cells are connected in series. The positive terminal of one cell is connected to the negative terminal of the next. The voltage of the battery is the sum of the voltages of the cells. You connect two cells in this way when you insert them into a flashlight. The total voltage of a battery is found by adding the voltages of the individual cells. If you use two 1.5-volt cells in your flashlight, the total voltage is 3 volts.

Wet Cells and Dry Cells There are two kinds of electrochemical cells: dry cells and wet cells. An electrochemical cell in which the electrolyte is a liquid is a **wet cell**. Volta's battery consisted of wet cells because the electrolyte was salt water. The six-volt automobile battery in Figure 21B consists of three wet cells. In this case, the electrolyte is sulfuric acid. Twelve-volt batteries, which are more common, consist of six wet cells.

For many devices, it would not be convenient to have cells full of liquid that can spill or leak. Flashlights and many other devices use dry cells instead. A **dry cell** is an electrochemical cell in which the electrolyte is not really dry, but a paste. The dry cell in Figure 21A consists of a zinc can with a carbon rod down the center. The can is filled with a thick electrolyte paste. Metal caps are attached at each end for terminals and the cell is wrapped in a plastic coating.

Dead and Rechargeable Batteries

An electrochemical cell will continue to produce a current until the electrodes and electrolyte are used up. During the reaction in an electrochemical cell, the original substances, known as the reactants, are changed into different substances. The new substances are known as products. A battery in which the reactants have run out is a dead battery.

Can you turn the products back into reactants in order to keep a battery going? In some cells, you can. In these cells the useless products can be converted back into the valuable reactants. Such cells are said to be rechargeable. A battery made of these cells is a **rechargeable battery.** Not every type of battery can be recharged. The electrodes must be carefully chosen so that a reverse reaction is possible.

A reverse chemical reaction in which products change into reactants does not happen on its own. Electrical energy, however, can cause the reaction. A rechargeable battery uses electric current to convert the products of its chemical reaction back into reactants.

Have you ever seen someone turn on a laptop computer without plugging it in? The battery on a laptop computer is rechargeable. Once the battery has run down, the computer can be plugged into a wall socket. Electrical energy from the wall socket causes a reverse reaction in the battery. When this reverse reaction is complete, the battery is fully charged.

In one type of rechargeable battery, the reactants are nickel and cadmium. Nickel-cadmium, or NiCad, batteries are popular in cordless and cellular telephones, radios, compact disc players, and other devices that require extended use.

Figure 22 Unlike other batteries that must be discarded after they become dead, rechargeable batteries can be re-used many times before they wear out.

Section 4 Review

1. Describe the components of an electrochemical cell and explain how they produce voltage.
2. Explain how cells are arranged to make a battery.
3. How does a wet cell differ from a dry cell?
4. What is a rechargeable battery?
5. **Thinking Critically   Applying Concepts** What would you tell an engineer who has suggested a design for a new battery using silver for both electrodes?

Science at Home

Can you revive a dead battery? Try the following with two old D cells and a flashlight. Test the flashlight with the old D cells and observe its brightness. Then ask a family member to remove the D cells and place them in direct sunlight to warm up. After an hour or more, use the cells to test the flashlight. How does the brightness of the bulb compare in the two tests? Explain to your family how a cell works. Then discuss what your observations indicate about the chemical reactions in the battery.

ELECTRICITY GROWS ON TREES

An electrochemical cell changes chemical energy into electrical energy. In this lab, you will practice the skill of drawing conclusions as you make a simple electrochemical cell starting with an apple.

Problem

How can you make a simple wet cell out of common household materials?

Materials

2 galvanized (zinc coated) nails
    about 10 cm long
2 pieces of copper about the same
    size as the nails
4 30-cm pieces of insulated wire with about
    2 cm of insulation removed from each end
2 marble-size lumps of clay
4 clothes pins (the "pinch" type with springs)
2 apples
calculator powered by one 1.5-volt dry cell

Procedure ✂

Part 1 Single Apple Power

1. Use the calculator to do some calculations to be sure it works.
2. Remove the dry cell from the calculator.
3. Stick a galvanized nail into an apple so that about three or four centimeters of the nail are showing. Stick a piece of stiff copper wire into the apple as well. **CAUTION:** *Take care handling sharp nails.*

4. Connect a piece of wire to the free end of the nail. Connect another piece of wire to the free end of the copper wire. Use clothespins to keep the connections tight.
5. Connect the free ends of the two wires to the open terminals of the calculator. Secure the connections with clothespins or pieces of clay.
6. Try using the calculator. If it doesn't work, be sure the connections are tight.
7. Reverse the connections. Again, be sure the connections are tight.

8. If you get the calculator to work, try using it to do some calculations. If not, continue on.

Part 2 Double Apple Power

9. Make another apple cell by repeating Steps 3 and 4 with a second apple, nail, piece of copper, and two pieces of wire.

10. Experiment with different ways of connecting the second cell until the calculator works. Once you get the calculator to work, switch the connections to the calculator and see if it still works.

11. Do you think the apple cell will work if you use two galvanized nails in each apple instead of using copper? Design an experiment to find out. Get your teacher's approval for your design, then carry out your experiment.

Analyze and Conclude

1. Draw circuit diagrams for the arrangements from Parts I and II.

2. Relate the parts of the apple cell to a typical electrochemical cell.

3. How does the calculator perform when powered by one apple? By two apples? How can you account for any differences?

4. Does the calculator work as well with the apple as it does with a dry cell?

5. Did the apple cell work with two nails? Explain why or why not.

6. What parts of the apple battery correspond to the positive end and the negative end of a dry cell? How do you know?

7. **Think About It** What was the result of reversing the connections? Why do you think this happened?

More to Explore

Are apples the only fruit that can be used to make enough electricity to power a calculator? Try oranges, lemons, tomatoes, or other fruits. Are there other instruments or appliances that can be powered with apple wet cells? Try small toys, electronic games, or electronic clocks. (*Hint:* The apple cells generate a low voltage.)

Disposing of Batteries—Safely

Americans use more than 2 billion batteries each year, for everything from flashlights and toys to cameras and computers. When batteries wear out, people throw most of them into the trash. The dead batteries end up buried in landfills or burned in incinerators.

The trouble with throwing away batteries is that they contain poisonous metals, such as mercury and cadmium. Mercury harms the nervous system, and cadmium can cause cancer. As batteries break down in landfills, they can release these metals into the soil. Eventually the metals can enter the water supply. Burning batteries in incinerators isn't any better, because the metals are released into the air as the batteries are burned. So what's the safest way to dispose of batteries?

The Issues

What Type of Battery Is Best? Alkaline batteries are used in toys, flashlights, radios, and watches. These batteries contain mercury. Even though there are some rechargeable alkaline batteries, most are thrown away once they are dead.

Nickel-cadmium (Ni-Cad) batteries are often used in hand-held video games and cordless telephones. These batteries contain cadmium. Ni-Cad batteries are rechargeable. One Ni-Cad battery can last as long as 12 single-use alkaline batteries. Yet they still don't last forever. Eventually they wear out and must be disposed of.

Where Should People Dispose of Batteries? Health experts say that batteries should be collected separately from ordinary trash and disposed of in secure, hazardous-waste landfills. These sites have clay or other materials underneath the waste to stop poisons from leaking into soil and water.

Some cities collect batteries at collection centers. Some stores also provide for special disposal or recycling. However, even when battery collection is offered, many people throw batteries into the trash simply because it's easier.

What Can People Do? Some government officials want laws that require manufacturers to reduce the amount of poisonous metals in batteries. At present, most states do not have such a law. In the last 20 years, manufacturers have lowered the amount of mercury used in alkaline batteries by 70 percent.

Local governments could fine people who don't follow the rules for disposal of batteries. But enforcing battery disposal rules would be expensive. It also would involve checking everyone's trash—a violation of people's privacy. A few states do require battery manufacturers to collect and recycle batteries. But this process is costly for companies and results in higher prices for batteries.

While people search for solutions, batteries continue to pile up.

You Decide

1. Identify the Problem
In your own words, explain the problem of safe battery disposal.

2. Analyze the Options
Examine the pros and cons of changing disposal regulations and changing the materials used to make batteries. In each case, who would the change affect?

3. Find a Solution
Your community is debating the problem of battery disposal. Take a position and write a speech supporting your opinion.

SECTION 1 — Electricity, Magnetism, and Motion

Key Ideas
◆ A magnetic field exerts a force on a wire carrying current, causing the wire to move.
◆ A galvanometer uses the magnetic force on a current-carrying wire to turn a pointer on a scale. The scale can then be used to measure current.
◆ An electric motor converts electrical energy into mechanical energy.

Key Terms
energy
electrical energy
mechanical energy
galvanometer

electric motor
commutator
brushes
armature

SECTION 2 — Generating Electric Current

Key Ideas
◆ A current is induced in a wire in a moving or changing magnetic field.
◆ Current that moves in one direction only is called direct current. Current that reverses direction is called alternating current.
◆ A generator converts mechanical energy into electric energy.
◆ Mechanical energy is required to move a turbine. That energy can be supplied by falling water, the burning of fossil fuels, the wind, the sun, the tides, or steam from within Earth.

Key Terms
electromagnetic
  induction
alternating current
direct current
electric generator

slip rings
turbine
renewable resource
nonrenewable
  resource

SECTION 3 — Using Electric Power

Key Ideas
◆ Power is the rate at which energy is converted.
◆ A transformer increases or decreases voltage.
◆ The voltage of alternating current can be stepped up and stepped down.

Key Terms
power
transformer

step-up transformer
step-down transformer

SECTION 4 — Batteries

INTEGRATING **CHEMISTRY**

Key Ideas
◆ An electrochemical cell consists of two different metals, called electrodes, and a substance through which charges can flow, called an electrolyte.
◆ In a battery, two or more electrochemical cells are connected in series to increase the voltage.

Key Terms
chemical energy
chemical reaction
electrochemical cell
electrode

electrolyte
terminal
battery
wet cell

dry cell
rechargeable
  battery

Organizing Information

Concept Map Copy the concept map about electromagnetism onto a separate sheet of paper. Then complete the concept map and add a title. (For more about concept maps, see the Skills Handbook.)

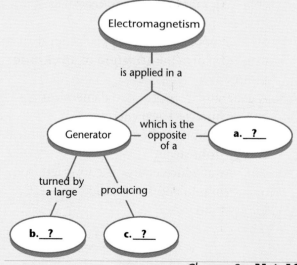

Reviewing Content

For more review of key concepts, see the Interactive Student Tutorial CD-ROM.

Multiple Choice

Choose the letter of the answer that best completes each statement.

1. Electrical energy is converted into mechanical energy in a
   a. motor.　　　　b. generator.
   c. transformer.　d. battery.
2. Mechanical energy is converted into electrical energy in a
   a. motor.　　　　b. galvanometer.
   c. generator.　　d. commutator.
3. Power is equal to
   a. energy × time.
   b. voltage × current.
   c. energy × current.
   d. current ÷ voltage.
4. A device that changes the voltage of alternating current is a
   a. transformer.　b. motor.
   c. generator.　　d. galvanometer.
5. The metal plates in an electrochemical cell are called
   a. electrolytes.　b. electrodes.
   c. armatures.　　d. brushes.

True or False

If the statement is true, write true. If it is false, change the underlined word or words to make the statement true.

6. The production of an electric current by a changing magnetic field is known as <u>induction</u>.
7. Several loops of wire wrapped around an iron core form the <u>armature</u> of an electric motor.
8. A <u>generator</u> converts stored chemical energy into electrical energy.
9. Large generators often get their mechanical energy from <u>steam</u>.
10. The rate at which energy is converted from one form into another is called <u>kilowatt-hours</u>.

Checking Concepts

11. How is a galvanometer similar to a motor? How is it different?
12. What is the role of the commutator and brushes in an electric motor?
13. Describe the operation of an AC generator.
14. Compare and contrast alternating and direct current.
15. What is the purpose of a turbine in generating electricity?
16. What are the pros and cons of coal, wind power, and nuclear power?
17. Explain how transformers are used to carry electricity from the utility company to your home.
18. What is a chemical reaction? How are chemical reactions related to batteries?
19. **Writing to Learn** Sometimes you may think that everything that could possibly be invented already exists. Many people thought the same thing during the 1800s. Write an article for a modern newspaper describing new uses for generators and motors.

Thinking Critically

20. **Problem Solving** The voltage of a car battery is 12 volts. When the car is started, the battery produces a 40-amp current. How much power does it take to start the car?
21. **Comparing and Contrasting** Compare the cost of using the following two bulbs. Assume that each one is used for 5 hours a day for 360 days per year. The cost of electricity is 8 cents/kWh.
    a. A 100-watt light bulb that costs $1.00
    b. A fluorescent bulb that costs $9 but provides equal brightness with only 20 watts
22. **Applying Concepts** How could you modify a battery to produce a higher voltage?
23. **Making Diagrams** Make a diagram of a wire loop in a magnetic field. Show how the direction of a current in the wire is related to the direction of rotation of the loop

Applying Skills

Use the illustration to answer Questions 24–26.

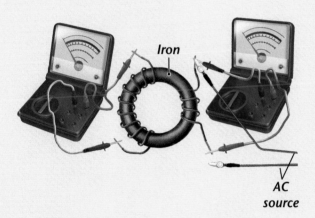

Iron

AC source

24. **Classifying** What type of transformer is shown in the illustration? How do you know?

25. **Inferring** Which coil is the primary coil and which is the secondary coil?

26. **Predicting** What will the two voltmeters show when the circuit on the right side of the diagram is completed?

CHAPTER PROJECT 3

Performance **Assessment**

Project Wrap Up Present the results of your energy audit to the class in a visual format. You might make a bar, circle, or line graph showing the appliances and the energy they used. What appliance uses the most electrical energy in a week? Compare the appliances that are rated at 800 watts and higher. What do they have in common? How might this conclusion be helpful to a consumer who is interested in paying the least for electricity?

Record and Reflect In your journal, write about how you calculated energy use. What problems did you have? What information couldn't you collect?

Test Preparation

Use these questions to prepare for standardized tests.

Study the table. Then answer Questions 27–30.

Appliance	Power (W)
Stove	6,000
Clothes dryer	5,400
Water heater	4,500
Washing machine	1,200
Hair dryer	1,200
Iron	1,100
Coffee maker	1,000
Food processor	500

27. If all of these appliances were used for one hour, which would use the greatest amount of energy?
   a. food processor b. hair dryer
   c. clothes dryer d. stove

28. Which device uses energy at the same rate as ten 100-watt light bulbs?
   a. food processor
   b. coffee maker
   c. washing machine
   d. stove

29. If standard household voltage is 120 volts, what is the current through the stove?
   a. 0.05 amp
   b. 20 amps
   c. 50 amps
   d. 750 amps

30. An electric company charges $0.25 for every kilowatt-hour of energy. How much does it cost to run a water heater for 2 hours?
   a. $0.50 b. $1.13
   c. $2.25 d. $4.50

CHAPTER

4 Electronics

WEB
ACTIVITY
www.phschool.com

 SECTION **1** **Electronic Signals and Semiconductors**

Discover **Can You Send Information With a Flashlight?**
Sharpen Your Skills **Communicating**
Real-World Lab **Design a Battery Sensor**

 SECTION **2** **Electronic Communication**

Discover **Are You Seeing Spots?**

 SECTION **3** **Computers**

Discover **How Fast Are You?**
Sharpen Your Skills **Calculating**
Skills Lab **The Penny Computer**

This red wolf wears a collar that sends radio tracking signals to naturalists.

4

Bits and Bytes

Red wolves are very intelligent animals, but their survival is threatened. They may benefit from the work of scientists who track their movements with electronic equipment. In a similar way, you benefit from electronics every day. Both a comfortable air-conditioned building and an airmail letter from thousands of miles away are made possible by electronics. In this chapter you will learn about the devices that make computers possible, how computers work, and how they are used. As you complete the chapter, you will identify a new computer use, or application.

Your Goal To study an existing computer application and then propose and detail a new application.

Your project must
- ◆ show what the existing computer application does and explain its benefits
- ◆ explain how data are received and transformed by the computer
- ◆ describe each step that occurs as your new application runs

Get Started Brainstorm with your classmates about existing computer applications. Make a list of devices that use programmed information, such as clock radios, automated bank teller machines, and grocery store bar-code scanners.

Check Your Progress You'll be working on this project as you study this chapter. To keep your project on track, look for Check Your Progress boxes at the following points.
Section 1 Review, page 118: Research a computer application.
Section 3 Review, page 135: Develop a new computer application.

Wrap Up At the end of this chapter (page 145), you will present both the existing application and your new one to the class.

Electronic Signals and Semiconductors

DISCOVER ••• ACTIVITY ••••

Can You Send Information With a Flashlight?

1. Write a short sentence on a sheet of paper.

2. Morse code is a language that uses dots and dashes to convey information. Convert your sentence to dots and dashes using the International Morse Code chart at the right.

3. Turn a flashlight on and off quickly to represent dots. Leave the flashlight on a little longer to represent dashes. Practice using the flashlight for several different letters.

4. Use the flashlight to transmit your sentence to a partner. Ask your partner to translate your message and write down your sentence.

International Morse Code	A ·—	B —···	C —·—·	D —··	E ·
F ··—·	G ——·	H ····	I ··	J ·———	K —·—	L ·—··
M ——	N —·	O ———	P ·——·	Q ——·—	R ·—·	S ···
T —	U ··—	V ···—	W ·——	X —··—	Y —·——	Z ——··

Think It Over

Inferring Were you able to transmit information using light? How does your light message differ from the same message read aloud?

GUIDE FOR READING

♦ How is electronics related to electricity?

♦ What are analog and digital signals?

♦ How are semiconductors used in solid-state devices?

Reading Tip As you read, write a phrase describing each boldfaced term in your own words.

No matter where you live, you can't go far without seeing an electronic device. Your radio and television are electronic, and so are video cameras and telephones. Making popcorn in a microwave oven requires electronics. Even an automobile engine won't run without electronics.

Most of these devices are plugged into a source of electric current. You might wonder, then, why they aren't just called electrical devices. The difference between electrical and electronic devices is in the way that they use electric current.

Electricity Versus Electronics

So far in this book, you have been learning about electricity. In electrical devices, a continuous flow of electric current is required. A light bulb is an example of an electrical device because it relies on a continuous supply of electric current.

Electronics is the use of electricity to control, communicate, and process information. **Electronics treats electric currents as a means of carrying information.** If you did the Discover activity, you turned a beam of light on and off to send a message. You controlled the current by turning a flashlight on and off. You used the flashlight as an electronic device.

Figure 1 Electronic controls can be found in many electrical appliances.

Electronic Signals

Electronics is based on electronic signals. An **electronic signal** is a varying electric current that represents information. Anything that can be measured or numbered, whether it is electrical or not, can be converted to a signal.

There are two basic kinds of electronic signals: analog signals and digital signals. Thermometers are a good example to show the difference between digital and analog.

Analog and Digital Devices You may have noticed that there are two different kinds of thermometers. One kind shows temperature as the height of a liquid in a tube. The height of the liquid rises and falls smoothly with the temperature. This is an analog thermometer. The other kind of thermometer is the kind you might see in front of a bank. It is called a digital thermometer. It shows a number that represents the temperature.

The number on this type of outdoor digital thermometer is constant for a few minutes, or perhaps several hours. Then the number changes suddenly by a whole degree. You probably know that the temperature doesn't really change so suddenly. But the thermometer can only show the temperature to the nearest degree, and so the temperature seems to jump.

Analog and Digital Signals The terms analog and digital are usually applied to the transmission of information using electric current. Just as there are two ways of representing temperature, there are two kinds of electronic signals. In **analog signals,** a current is varied smoothly to represent information. **An analog signal is created when a current is smoothly changed or varied.**

Figure 2 These two thermometers are examples of analog and digital devices. *Applying Concepts What do digital and analog clocks look like?*

In **digital signals,** pulses of current are used to represent information. **A digital signal consists of a current that changes in steps.** Rather than changing smoothly to represent information, a digital signal carries information in pulses. If you did the Discover activity, you used pulses of light to represent letters.

Sound Recordings The photos in Figure 3 show an analog sound recording. When you play an old plastic record, a needle runs along a spiral groove. As the needle moves back and forth in the groove, it creates a small electric current. This current matches the wavy pattern of the groove in the record.

The current produced by the needle forms an analog signal. The signal continuously changes as it copies the information on the record. The analog signal is fed into an amplifier and then into a speaker, which changes the signal back into sound.

As you can see in Figure 4, a CD, or compact disc, is very different. It contains microscopic holes, called pits. The level areas between the pits are called flats. These pits and flats are arranged in a spiral, like the groove on a record. Although you can't tell from the photograph, the spiral on a compact disc is divided into pieces of equal length. The arrangement of pits and flats within each piece of the spiral is a code. Each piece of this code represents the volume of sound at one instant.

Figure 3 The magnified photo shows the needle of a record player moving along the groove of a record. *Interpreting Photos Why does the smooth shape of the groove represent an analog signal?*

MOZART
CLARINET CONCERTO IN A MAJOR (K. 622)
Allegro
Adagio
Rondo

STPL 511.110   Side 1
Rec. in Stuttgart
29:46 min.

Jost MICHAELS, clarinet

Westphalia Symphony Orchestra
HUBERT REICHERT, conductor
STPL 511.110 A
(S-203-A)

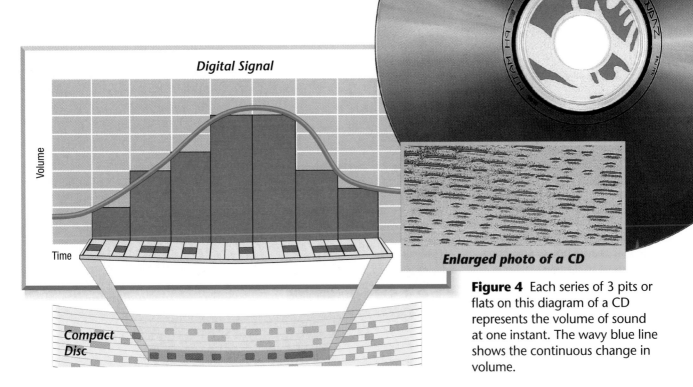

Digital Signal

Volume

Time

Enlarged photo of a CD

Compact Disc

Figure 4 Each series of 3 pits or flats on this diagram of a CD represents the volume of sound at one instant. The wavy blue line shows the continuous change in volume.

When the CD is played, it spins around, and a beam of light scans the pits and flats. Like the bar code scanner used in a supermarket, this beam produces tiny flashes of light. The light flashes are then converted to pulses of electric current, or a digital signal. The digital signal is fed into an amplifier and then a speaker, where it is changed back into sound.

☑ *Checkpoint* *What are the two types of electronic signals?*

Semiconductors

How can you control a voltage in order to transmit analog or digital signals? After all, you have learned that current flows continuously through a conductor, but does not flow at all through an insulator. Yet to transmit an electronic signal you need to be able to vary the current through a circuit. When you vary current, you use a semiconductor.

A **semiconductor** is a material that conducts current better than insulators but not as well as conductors. A semiconductor conducts electricity only under certain conditions.

How can a material conduct electricity only under certain conditions? Silicon and other semiconductors are elements that have extremely high resistance in their pure forms. However, if atoms of other elements are added to semiconductors, they conduct current much more easily. By controlling the number and type of atoms added, scientists produce two types of semiconductors. They combine these two types of semiconductors in layers. This structure allows the delicate control of current needed for electronic devices. Such control is impossible with true conductors.

Figure 5 The electrical resistance of pure silicon, shown here, is reduced by adding atoms of other elements to it.

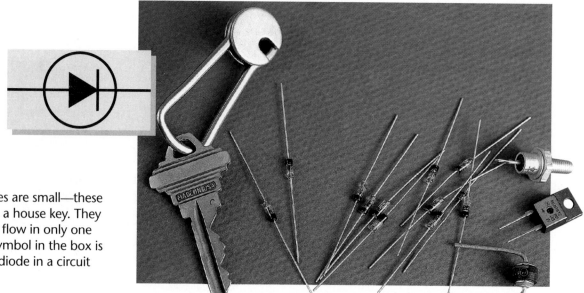

Figure 6 Diodes are small—these are smaller than a house key. They allow current to flow in only one direction. The symbol in the box is used to show a diode in a circuit diagram.

Solid-State Components

A **solid-state component** is part of a circuit in which a signal is controlled by a solid material, such as a semiconductor. **The two types of semiconductors can be combined in different ways to produce different solid-state components. These components include diodes and transistors.** Since the 1950s, solid-state components have become dominant in electronic devices.

Diodes A solid-state component that consists of layers of the two types of semiconductors joined together is a **diode.** A diode allows current to flow in one direction only. If you connect a diode in a circuit in one direction, current will flow. But if you turn the diode around, current will not flow.

Recall that there are two types of current: alternating current and direct current. Your home uses alternating current. A battery-operated game uses direct current. Electronic devices are designed to run on only one type of current. However, you can plug some direct-current devices into an alternating-current outlet if you have a converter. A converter does not change the way the device operates. Instead, a converter changes, or converts, the current.

An alternating current reverses direction over and over again. When a diode is placed in a circuit with alternating current, the diode allows current to flow only when it is moving in one direction. So a converter allows only part of the alternating current to flow—the part flowing in one direction. Alternating current goes into the converter, but direct current comes out.

Transistors When a layer of either type of semiconductor is sandwiched between two layers of the other type of semiconductor, a transistor is formed. A **transistor** carries out one of two

Figure 7 Transistors come in a variety of shapes and sizes. The symbol for a transistor is shown in the box. *Applying Concepts What is a transistor?*

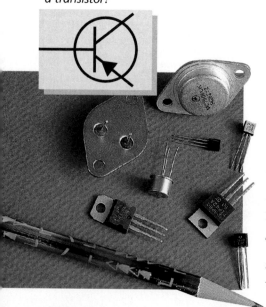

functions: it either amplifies an electronic signal or switches current on and off.

When electronic signals are sent, they gradually grow weak. When they are received, signals must be amplified, or made stronger, so that we can use them. Transistors revolutionized the electronics industry by making amplifiers much cheaper and more reliable.

When a transistor acts as a switch, it either lets current through or cuts it off. Millions of transistors that act as switches are what make computers work.

Integrated Circuits Single transistors have low cost and long lives. These advantages were multiplied by the invention of the integrated circuit. An **integrated circuit** is a circuit that has been manufactured on a tiny slice of semiconductor known as a chip. A chip smaller than 0.5 centimeters on each side can contain hundreds of thousands of components, such as diodes, transistors, and resistors. Electronic signals flow through integrated circuits at tremendous speeds because the various components are so close together. On some chips, the space between two components can be one-fiftieth as thick as a human hair. The high speed of signals and small size of integrated circuits make possible devices from video games to spacecraft.

☑ *Checkpoint* *What is a solid-state component?*

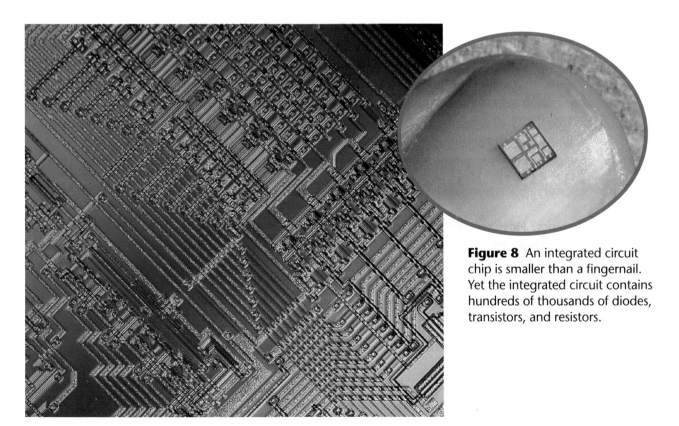

Figure 8 An integrated circuit chip is smaller than a fingernail. Yet the integrated circuit contains hundreds of thousands of diodes, transistors, and resistors.

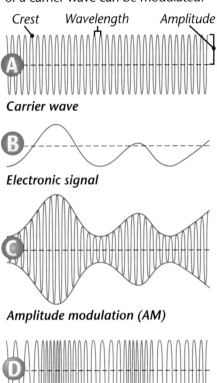

Figure 16 Amplitude or frequency of a carrier wave can be modulated.

Carrier wave

Electronic signal

Amplitude modulation (AM)

Frequency modulation (FM)

Amplitude and Frequency Modulation All waves have certain basic characteristics. Figure 16A shows a simple wave moving from left to right. The high points are called crests and the low points are called troughs. Waves are described in terms of two quantities, amplitude and frequency. The **amplitude** is the height from the center line to a crest or trough. The **frequency** of a wave is the number of waves passing a given point each second.

The amplitude and frequency of an electromagnetic wave can be changed, or modulated, to carry an electronic signal. The wave that is modulated, shown in Figure 16A, is called the carrier wave. Figure 16B shows an electronic signal. In this case, the signal is an analog signal in which the strength, or amplitude, of an electric current changes.

The carrier wave can be modulated to match the electronic signal in two different ways, as shown in Figures 16C and 16D. One way is to change the amplitude of the carrier wave to match that of the signal. This process is known as **amplitude modulation (AM).** The other way is to change the frequency of the carrier wave to match the amplitude of the signal. Then the space between the waves varies with the strength of the signal. This process is known as **frequency modulation (FM).**

Figure 17 In radio transmission, sounds are converted to electronic signals that are carried by electromagnetic waves.

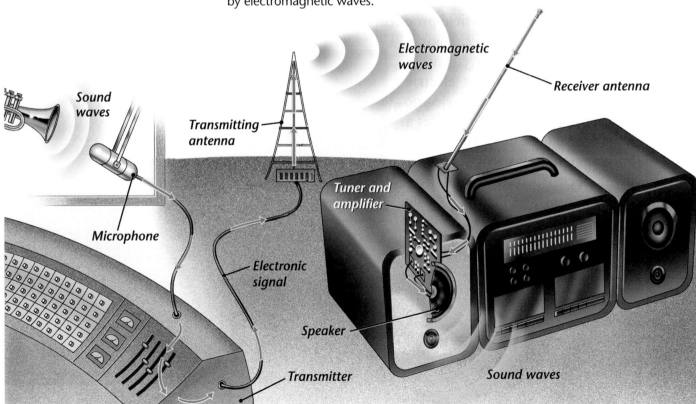

Radio

Voices or music on an AM or FM radio station are electronic signals carried by an electromagnetic wave. But where do the sounds you hear come from?

Transmission The process begins at a radio station, where sounds are converted into an electronic signal. If a musician plays into a microphone at a radio station, the sound waves produce a varying electric current. This current is an analog signal that represents the sound waves. It is sometimes called an audio signal.

The electronic audio signal is then sent to a transmitter. The transmitter amplifies the signal and combines it with an electronic carrier signal. The signal is then sent to an antenna, which sends out electromagnetic waves in all directions.

Reception Your radio has its own antenna that receives the electromagnetic waves from the radio station. The carrier wave has a specific frequency. You tune in to the wave by selecting that frequency on your radio. Your radio amplifies the signal and separates it from the carrier wave. The signal is then sent to the radio's speaker, which is the reverse of a microphone. The speaker converts the electronic signal back into sound.

☑ *Checkpoint* *What is an audio signal?*

Television

Electromagnetic waves can be used to carry images as well as sound. The transmission of the images and sounds on television is very similar to that of radio sounds.

Transmission Television signals are usually sent from transmitting antennas on the ground. Sometimes, however, the signal is blocked by the landscape of an area or by nearby buildings. Or sometimes a transmitter cannot reach homes that are too far away. To solve these problems, local cable television networks have been developed. These networks distribute television signals through cables from a central receiver to individual homes.

Communications satellites are also used to relay television signals. A communications satellite orbits Earth, always staying above the same point on the ground. These satellites receive signals from one part of the planet and transmit them to another almost instantly. This enables you to watch events from around the world as they occur.

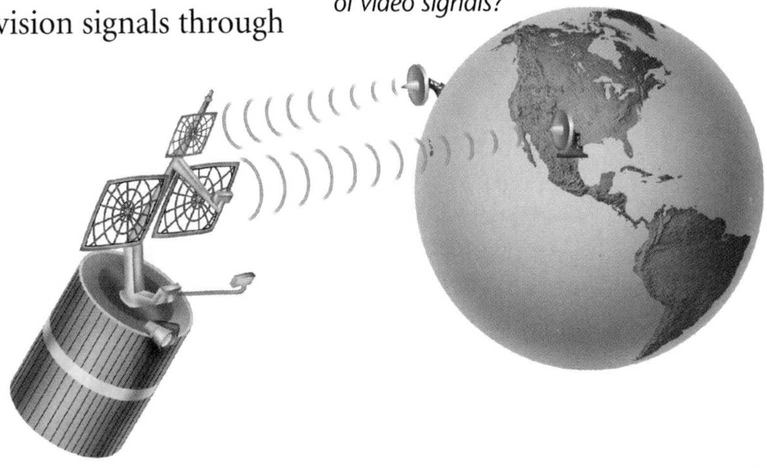

Figure 18 A communications satellite orbits Earth at the same rate at which Earth spins. Therefore it stays above the same point on Earth.
Applying Concepts How are communications satellites involved in the transmission of video signals?

How Fast Are You?

1. Write out ten math problems involving the addition or subtraction of two two-digit numbers.

2. Switch lists with a friend.

3. Take turns timing how long it takes each of you to solve the ten problems by hand.

4. Then time how long it takes each of you to solve the ten problems using a calculator. What is the time difference? Is there a difference in accuracy?

Think It Over

Inferring What are the advantages of using an electronic device to complete calculations?

GUIDE FOR READING

◆ How is information stored and processed in a computer?

◆ How is computer hardware different from computer software?

Reading Tip As you read, use the headings to make an outline about how computers work.

Figure 21 You may never have seen an abacus, but these devices can be used to perform complex calculations.

Over two thousand years ago, the first calculator was invented. But it was not what you may think. This calculating device is called an abacus. People use an abacus to count by sliding beads along strings.

In the United States, mechanical adding machines and abacuses have generally been replaced by electronic calculators and computers. Although the development of computers has occurred in less than a century, computers have become commonplace.

What Is a Computer?

A **computer** is an electronic device that stores, processes, and retrieves information. One of the reasons that computers can process and store so much information is that they do not store information in the same form that you see it—numbers, letters, and pictures. **Computer information is represented in the binary system.** The **binary system** uses combinations of just two digits, 0 and 1. Although computers can use analog signals, almost all modern computers are digital.

INTEGRATING MATHEMATICS You may be wondering how large numbers can be represented using only series of 1's and 0's. Begin by thinking about the numbers with which you are more familiar. You are used to using the base-10 number system. Each place value in a number represents the number 10 raised to some power. The digits 1 through 9 are then multiplied by the place value in each position. For example, the number 327 means 3×100 plus 2×10 plus 7×1.

Binary System

Place Values 8 4 2 1	Expanded Value		Base-10 Number
1 =	$(1 \times 1) =$	1 =	1
1 0 =	$(1 \times 2) + (0 \times 1) =$	2 + 0 =	2
1 1 =	$(1 \times 2) + (1 \times 1) =$	2 + 1 =	3
1 0 0 =	$(1 \times 4) + (0 \times 2) + (0 \times 1) =$	4 + 0 + 0 =	4
1 0 1 =	$(1 \times 4) + (0 \times 2) + (1 \times 1) =$	4 + 0 + 1 =	5
1 0 1 0 =	$(1 \times 8) + (0 \times 4) + (1 \times 2) + (0 \times 1) =$	8 + 0 + 2 + 0 =	10
1 0 1 1 =	$(1 \times 8) + (0 \times 4) + (1 \times 2) + (1 \times 1) =$	8 + 0 + 2 + 1 =	11
1 1 1 1 =	$(1 \times 8) + (1 \times 4) + (1 \times 2) + (1 \times 1) =$	8 + 4 + 2 + 1 =	15

Figure 22 Each place value in the binary system is double the value to its right. In this table, you see the binary numbers representing the base-10 numbers 1, 2, 3, 4, 5, 10, 11, and 15. *Interpreting Charts What is your age in the binary system?*

The binary system is similar to the base-10 number system, except that the base number is 2. Notice in Figure 22 that the place values begin with 1, 2, 4, and 8 instead of 1, 10, 100, and 1,000. In the binary system, only the numbers 0 and 1 are multiplied by each place value.

Each 1 or 0 in the binary system is called a **bit,** short for **bi**nary dig**it**. Arrangements of eight bits are called **bytes.** Computer memories are rated in kilobytes (one thousand bytes), megabytes (one million bytes), or even gigabytes (one billion bytes).

☑ *Checkpoint* What two digits are used in the binary system?

Computer Memory

There are many ways to record 0's and 1's. The pits and flats on a CD can represent 0's and 1's. CDs can store not just music, but any kind of data. Computers can also use magnetic tapes to store information. Magnetic tapes, such as video and audio tapes, record information by changing the arrangement of magnetic domains. The magnetic domains can be oriented in one direction to represent 1's, and in the opposite direction to represent 0's.

Computers also use integrated circuits, or chips. Chips contain thousands of tiny circuits with transistors that act as switches. A switch in the off position represents a 0 and a switch in the on position represents a 1. One chip may consist of as many as 16 million switches or bits.

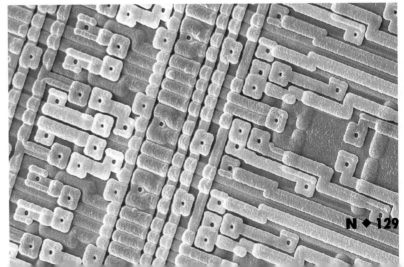

Figure 23 Electronic switches are shown in this enlarged view. They are part of a chip that can store over 500,000 bits of information.

EXPLORING Computer Hardware

A computer system has several basic physical parts that are used to enter data into the computer, process the data, and retrieve information out of the computer.

Input Devices

The computer gathers data by means of input devices such as a keyboard, mouse, scanner, joystick, microphone, light pen, scanner, or touch-sensitive screen.

Modem

A modem, which connects a computer to a telephone line, can serve as both an input and an output device.

Monitor

Keyboard

Microphone

Modem

Scanner

Mouse

Light pen

Computer Hardware

The physical parts that allow a computer to receive, store, and present information make up the computer's hardware. **Computer hardware** refers to the permanent components of the computer. **Computer hardware includes a central processing unit, input devices, output devices, and memory storage devices.** Identify the different devices as you read *Exploring Computer Hardware.*

The central processing unit serves as the brain of a computer. The **central processing unit,** or CPU, directs the operation of the computer, performs logical operations and calculations, and stores information.

Data are fed to a CPU by an **input device.** There are several different types of input devices. The one most familiar to you is probably the keyboard. Other input devices are shown in *Exploring Computer Hardware.*

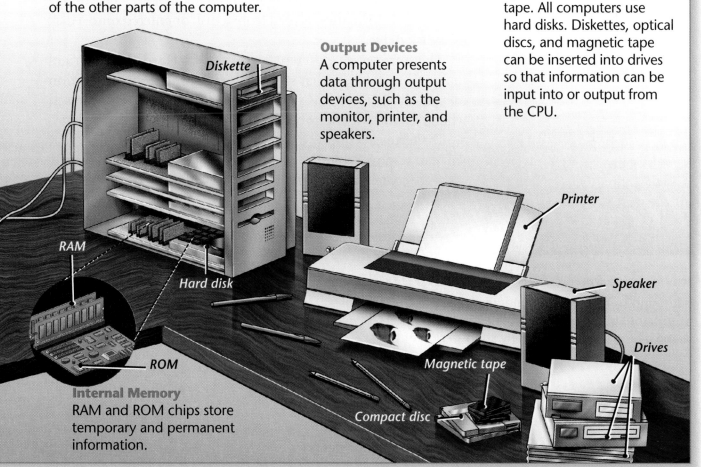

Central Processing Unit (CPU)
The CPU is the control center of the computer. The CPU processes and stores information, and coordinates the functions of the other parts of the computer.

Diskette

Output Devices
A computer presents data through output devices, such as the monitor, printer, and speakers.

External Memory
Information can be stored on hard disks, diskettes, optical discs, and magnetic tape. All computers use hard disks. Diskettes, optical discs, and magnetic tape can be inserted into drives so that information can be input into or output from the CPU.

RAM

Hard disk

Printer

ROM

Speaker

Internal Memory
RAM and ROM chips store temporary and permanent information.

Magnetic tape

Drives

Compact disc

Data from a computer are presented on an **output device.** A computer monitor, on which you view information, is the most familiar output device. Other output devices are shown in *Exploring Computer Hardware.*

Memory Devices

Computers store information in their memory. There are two general types of computer memory, internal and external. Chips on the main circuit board within the CPU are referred to as internal memory. **Random Access Memory (RAM)** is the temporary storage area for data while the computer is operating. Information stored in RAM is lost when the computer is turned off.

Information the computer needs to operate properly is stored in **Read Only Memory (ROM).** The CPU can read these data but cannot change them. Information in ROM is permanently stored and is not lost when the computer is turned off.

Neither RAM nor ROM allows you to save information when you turn your computer off. For that reason, devices outside the main CPU circuit are used to store information. They are called external memory. The most widely used form of external storage is the disk. Information is read from a disk or entered onto a disk by a **disk drive.**

There are several different types of disks. **Hard disks** are rigid magnetic metal disks that stay inside the computer. Information on a hard disk remains in the computer and can be accessed whenever you use the computer.

Diskettes, or floppy disks, are thin, round plastic disks that you can remove from the computer and carry with you. Floppy disks are coated with magnetic material laid in circles. If you have

The Development of Computers

Although some modern computers can fit in the palm of your hand, this wasn't always the case. Computers have come a long way in a relatively short period of time.

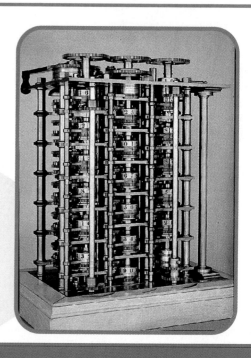

1823

The Difference Engine

British mathematician Charles Babbage designed the first computer, called the Difference Engine. It was a mechanical computing device that had more than 50,000 moving parts. For a later computer of Babbage's, Ada Lovelace wrote what is considered the first computer program.

1800	1850

1890

Census Counting Machine

Herman Hollerith constructed a machine that processed information by allowing electric current to pass through holes in punch cards. With Hollerith's machine, the United States census of 1890 was completed in one fourth the time needed for the 1880 census.

used such a diskette, you may be confused by the term *floppy*. This is because the floppy disk is encased in a hard, square plastic case for protection. If you slide the metal portion of the case to the side, you can see the floppy disk inside.

Another type of memory is an optical disc, also called a compact disc. An **optical disc** is a disc on which information is written and read by lasers. Optical discs can hold much greater amounts of information than diskettes. They are commonly used for video games. They also hold reference materials such as encyclopedias, magazines, and videos. Such optical discs are called CD-ROMs (Compact Disc—Read-Only Memory).

☑ *Checkpoint* **What is read-only memory (ROM)?**

In 1953, there were only about 100 computers in the entire world. Today, there are hundreds of millions of computers in businesses, homes, government offices, schools, and stores. Select one of the early forms of the computer. Write a newspaper article introducing it and its applications to the public.

1946
ENIAC

The first American-built computer was developed by the United States Army. The Electronic Numerical Integrator and Calculator, or ENIAC, consisted of thousands of vacuum tubes and filled an entire warehouse. To change the program, programmers had to rewire the entire machine.

1900	1950	2000

1939
Binary System

American physicists John V. Atanasoff and Clifford Berry produced a working model of a computer based on the binary system. They recognized that the digits 1 and 0 could be easily represented by electronic components.

1974
Personal Computers

The first personal computer (PC) went on the market. Today's personal computer is 400 times faster than ENIAC, 3,000 times lighter, and several million dollars cheaper.

Computer Software

A computer needs a set of instructions that tell it what to do. **A program is a detailed set of instructions that directs the computer hardware to perform operations on stored information.** Computer programs are called **computer software.** Whenever you use a word processor, solve mathematical problems, or play a computer game, a computer program is instructing the computer to perform in a certain way.

One category of computer software is called the operating system of the computer. An operating system is a set of basic instructions that keep a computer running. Perhaps you have heard of the operating software known as DOS, or disk operating system. Unix is another example of operating software.

A second category of software is usually called applications software. Applications are particular tasks that a computer may carry out. These programs are grouped by their function, such as word processing, graphics, games, or simulations.

☑ *Checkpoint* *What is a computer program?*

Computer Programming

People who program computers are called computer programmers. **Computer programmers** use computer languages that convert input information into instructions that the CPU can understand. You may have heard the names of some computer languages, such as Fortran, Basic, C, and COBOL. Each language is designed for a specific purpose. Fortran, for example, allows users to complete complex calculations. It is not, however, practical for word processing.

Programmers create software by using a step-by-step development process. First, they outline exactly what the program will do. Second, they develop a flowchart. A flowchart is a diagram showing the order of computer actions and data flow. Third, they write the instructions for the computer in a particular language. Complicated programs may contain millions of instructions. And finally, they test the program.

If the program does not work as the programmers intend, they *debug* it by identifying any problems with their logic. The term *bug* was applied to a mysterious malfunction in an early computer. Programmers discovered a moth in a vital electrical switch. Thereafter the programmers referred to problems as bugs and fixing problems as debugging.

Figure 24 Computer programmers develop software with all sorts of applications, from typing simple sentences to using simulators to train pilots and these oil rig operators.

Figure 25 Computers do not always take the form of desktop computers. Computer technology is used in devices as common as cameras and watches.

Computers at Work

Computer hardware and software are not always obvious. Just because you don't see an entire computer setup, you shouldn't assume a computer isn't involved. Do you wear a digital watch? If so, you are wearing a computer. Computer chips are used to control the timing of alarms and displays in digital watches.

Has a photographer ever taken your school picture? Computers and electronic sensors are used to monitor exposures in cameras. At the grocery store, computers are used to enter inventory bar codes into the cash register and add up your purchases. Computer chips are used to regulate engines in cars, monitor heating and cooling systems in buildings, and even to operate the locks on some doors. Look around. Computers are everywhere.

Section 3 Review

1. What is a computer? How does a computer store information?

2. How are computer hardware and software involved in the operation of a computer?

3. How do switches within a computer count to ten using binary code?

4. **Thinking Critically Classifying** Identify each of the following as an input device, output device, or both: keyboard, printer, diskette, scanner, touch-activated screen.

Check Your Progress

CHAPTER PROJECT 4

Choose a task that you would like to have done by a computer. Consider an activity such as mowing the lawn or watering the crops on a farm. Try to make your computer application original. Develop a series of steps that the computer would follow to complete the task. What input information is required? What is the resulting output from the computer? A flowchart diagram will help other students understand your new invention.

Skills Lab

Making Models

The Penny Computer

Computers can count only to 1! Computers use a binary number system that has only two digits, 0 and 1, to represent numbers. In a computer, a 0 is represented by a switch that is turned off, and a 1 by a switch that is turned on. You will make a model of a computer using pennies instead of switches.

Problem

How can pennies be used to model counting and adding in a computer?

Materials

15 pennies paper ruler
binary number table (Figure 22)

Procedure

Part 1 Binary Numbers

1. Review binary numbers. (See Figure 22 in this chapter.)
2. Before you use the computer, you need to learn the rules for counting with the penny code:
   - ◆ A heads-up penny represents the digit 1.
   - ◆ A tails-up penny represents the digit 0.

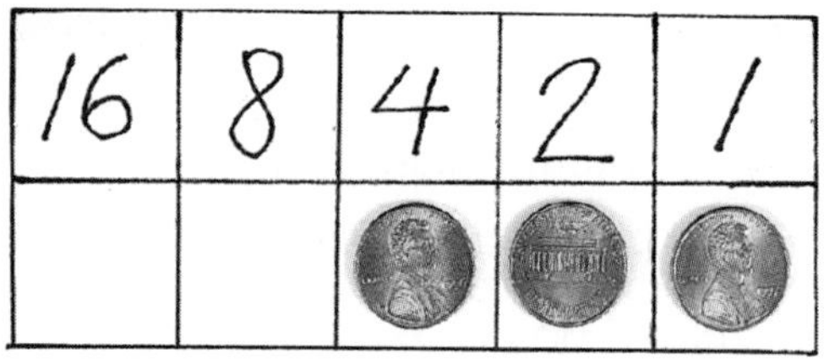

Figure 1

3. Examine Figure 1. The row of pennies represents a binary number. In your notebook, write the binary number represented by the row of pennies.
4. Convert this binary number to a base-10 number. Write the result in your notebook. Remember that the binary number 101 is equivalent to 5:
   $(1 \times 4) + (0 \times 2) + (1 \times 1) =$
   $4 + 0 + 1 = 5$
5. In your notebook, write the binary numbers 110, 111, 1000, 1001, and 10001.
6. Use pennies to represent these five binary numbers. Then convert the five binary numbers to their base-10 equivalents, and record.

Part 2 Adding with Binary Numbers

7. Learn the following rules for binary addition.

$$\begin{array}{r}0\\+0\\\hline 0\end{array}\qquad\begin{array}{r}1\\+0\\\hline 1\end{array}\qquad\begin{array}{r}1\\+1\\\hline 10\end{array}$$

The third rule may look odd, but remember that 10 in the binary system is equivalent to the number 2 in the base-10 system. The third rule shows you how to carry a 1 when adding binary numbers.

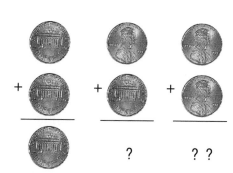

Figure 2

8. Using a heads-up penny for the digit 1, and a tails-up penny for the digit 0, the addition rules in Step 7 can be represented as shown in Figure 2. The first rule is complete. Use pennies to work out the other two. Copy the results in your notebook.

9. Look at Figure 3. It shows an addition problem done with the computer. Check that the arithmetic is done according to the rules you have learned. (Remember that you may have to carry a 1.)

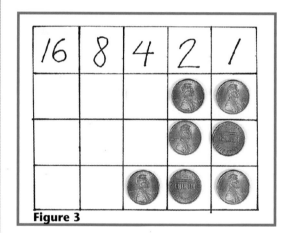

Figure 3

Part 3 Building a Binary Computer

10. Make a blank chart like the one in Figure 3. Be sure that each of the spaces in the three blank rows is large enough for a penny. This chart is your computer.

11. Put three pennies in the first blank row to represent the binary number 110.

12. Put three more pennies in the second row to represent the binary number 101.

13. Add together the two binary numbers. Use pennies to represent the sum.

14. Convert the three rows of pennies to base-10 numbers.

15. Use the base-10 numbers to check that you have done the problem correctly.

16. Next, use your computer to add the binary numbers 11 and 11. You will have to carry a 1 in two places. If you get the result 110, you have carried correctly.

17. Make up three other addition problems for your partner to solve. At least one of the binary numbers in each problem should have more than three digits. You will need to repeat Steps 10–15 each time. Write the problems in your notebook.

Analyze and Conclude

1. For the calculations you performed in Part 3, did you find the same results with the binary and base-10 systems?

2. What is the largest number that can be represented using 5 pennies? Explain.

3. How could you change your computer so you could represent larger numbers than your answer to Question 2? How could you represent 32 or 64 in the binary system? Use pennies to illustrate your answer.

4. **Think About It** In a computer, each on-off switch is called a bit. Eight bits make up 1 byte. How many pennies would be needed to model each byte? Suppose your home computer has a hard disk capacity of 10 gigabytes (10 billion bytes). How many pennies would be needed to model the number of bytes in the hard disk?

More to Explore

Find the rule that describes how your model can be used to double binary numbers. (*Hint:* You know that if you double the base-10 number 9, the answer is 18. What is 9 in binary? What is 18 in binary? Try other examples, and look for a pattern.) What is the relationship between a binary number and twice that number?

SECTION 4 The Information Superhighway

DISCOVER •••ACTIVITY•••

How Important Are Computers?

1. Obtain a local or national newspaper.
2. Look through the newspaper for articles that refer to computers, the Internet, the World Wide Web, or the information superhighway.
3. Write down the topics of the articles. For example, was the article about politics, painting, money, or computers?
4. Create a data table to show your results.

Think It Over

Inferring What can you infer about the kinds of information available through the computer? How much do you think people use computers to obtain information?

GUIDE FOR READING

◆ **What are the advantages of a computer network?**

◆ **What is the Internet?**

◆ **How can you use computers safely?**

Reading Tip Before you read, list five things that you know about the Internet. Add to your list after you read the section.

Because of the Internet, the world is at your fingertips! You can send an e-mail message to someone on the other side of the planet. Through the World Wide Web, information is yours for the searching as you prepare a school report. The news, sports scores, travel information, and weather reports are all available at any time. How is this possible? The answer is through the use of a computer connected to a network.

Computer Networks

You have traveled on a network of roads and highways that connects cities and towns. A **computer network** is a group of computers connected by cables or telephone lines. **A computer network allows people in different locations to share information and software.**

Figure 26 This is an artist's view of the information superhighway. *Forming Operational Definitions* How would you define *information superhighway*?

Figure 27 Cables connect computers in a local area network. People all over the world are connected by wide area networks such as the Internet.

There are two types of networks. A set of computers connected in one classroom or office building is known as a **local area network (LAN).** Computers connected across larger distances form a **wide area network (WAN).** In wide area networks, very powerful computers serve as a support connection for hundreds of less powerful computers.

The Internet

The most significant wide area network is the Internet. The **Internet** is a global network that links millions of computers in businesses, schools, and research organizations. **The Internet is a network of host computers that extends around the world.** You might say that the Internet is a network of networks. The Internet, along with other smaller networks, sometimes is called the information superhighway.

The Internet began in 1969 as a military communications system. Its purpose was to link computers used in military work. The links were designed so that communication would continue even if many computers were destroyed. In order for scientists to exchange data through their computers, colleges and universities were later added to the Internet.

Beginning in 1993, businesses were allowed to sell Internet connections to individuals. These businesses are known as Internet service providers (ISPs). With easy access available, the Internet has grown at an incredible rate. Its use for entertainment, shopping, and everyday information gathering completely overshadows its original purpose.

SCIENCE AND SOCIETY

When Seeing ISN'T Believing

The combination of computers and photography can make magic. A computer can turn the light, dark, and color areas in a photo into a code. By using the computer to change the code, a technician can change any part of a photo.

This way of working with photos is called digital manipulation. Fuzzy pictures can be made clearer and sharper. Colors can be brightened or completely changed. Tiny or hidden details can be made easier to see and understand. Old or stained photos can be made to look like new. Images of objects or people can even be added, removed, or moved around.

But some people worry that digital manipulation could be used to cheat or harm people. Are there ways to be informed and entertained by digital manipulation without being fooled by it?

The Issues

What Are the Dangers of Manipulated Photos?
It's nearly impossible to tell the difference between a digitally changed photo and an unchanged one. Suppose, for example, a photographer has one photo of your mother driving your family's car and another photo of your neighbor. With digital "magic," the photos could be combined to make it look like your neighbor is driving the car. With this capability, newspapers, magazines, and TV stations could mislead the public. Witnesses might use faked photos as evidence in court cases.

How Can People Protect Themselves?
Governments could pass laws against changing photographs. Such laws would be hard to enforce, however, because digital manipulation is so hard to detect. Laws might also make it difficult to use digital manipulation for useful purposes. And such laws might violate the right of free speech. Our courts consider photos a kind of speech, or expression.

Another option is for photographers or organizations to police themselves. They could write codes of conduct. The United States armed forces already have a code for photos (for instance, photos taken from military airplanes). Under this code, it is all right to make photos clearer digitally. But it is not all right to add, take away, or move around parts of a photo. Some photographers who work for newspapers have suggested a similar code for themselves.

Should Manipulated Photos Be Marked?
One safeguard might be to put a symbol on any digitally manipulated photo. That way viewers would be warned. But opponents point out that nearly every photo seen in newspapers and magazines is changed a little, usually just to make the colors more clear. If every photo had the symbol, people wouldn't be able to see the difference between a photo whose image had been made clearer and one in which something had been faked. People might stop trusting any photo.

You Decide

1. Identify the Problem
In your own words, describe the problems created by digital manipulation of photos.

2. Analyze the Options
List reasons for and against
a. passing a law that forbids changing any photo digitally.
b. letting photographers make their own code of conduct.
c. marking all digitally manipulated photos with a special symbol.

3. Find a Solution
You run a TV station. Your assistants want to use two digitally changed photos, one in a commercial and one in a news story. Will you let them use one, or both, or neither? Explain.

SECTION 1 — Electronic Signals and Semiconductors

Key Ideas

◆ Semiconductors are used to make solid-state devices such as integrated circuits.

Key Terms

electronics
electronic signal
analog signal
digital signal
semiconductor

solid-state component
diode
transistor
integrated circuit
vacuum tube

SECTION 2 — Electronic Communication

Key Ideas

◆ Sound is converted into electronic signals in radio and telephone transmitters.

◆ Electronic signals can be carried over long distances by electromagnetic waves.

Key Terms

electromagnetic
  wave
amplitude
frequency

amplitude
  modulation (AM)
frequency
  modulation (FM)
cathode-ray tube (CRT)

SECTION 3 — Computers

Key Ideas

◆ Computer hardware includes the central processing unit, input devices, output devices, and memory storage devices.

Key Terms

computer
binary system
bit
byte
computer hardware
central processing unit
input device
output device
random-access
  memory (RAM)

read-only memory
  (ROM)
disk drive
hard disk
diskette
optical disc
computer software
computer
  programmer

SECTION 4 — The Information Superhighway

Key Ideas

◆ Computers are connected by computer networks. The Internet is a network of host computers that extends around the world.

◆ Safe use of computer networks includes checking for viruses and using chat rooms with caution.

Key Terms

computer network
local area network (LAN)
wide area network (WAN)
Internet
World Wide Web
encryption

computer virus
chat room
intellectual property
freeware
shareware

Organizing Information

Flowchart Copy the flowchart about telephone communication onto a sheet of paper. Complete the flowchart by filling in the missing steps. (For more on flowcharts, see the Skills Handbook.)

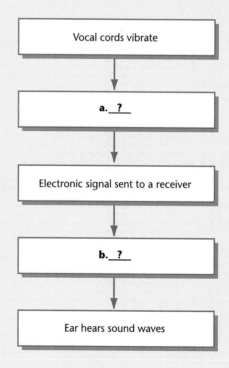

Vocal cords vibrate

↓

a. ?

↓

Electronic signal sent to a receiver

↓

b. ?

↓

Ear hears sound waves

Reviewing Content

 For more review of key concepts, see the Interactive Student Tutorial CD-ROM.

Multiple Choice

Choose the letter of the best answer.

1. A sandwich of 3 layers of semiconductor that is used to amplify an electric signal is known as a(n)
   a. diode.
   b. modem.
   c. transistor.
   d. integrated circuit.

2. A radio speaker
   a. converts sound to an electronic signal.
   b. converts an electronic signal to sound.
   c. places an electronic signal on an electromagnetic wave.
   d. controls the function of an electron gun.

3. An example of a computer output device is a
   a. printer.   b. keyboard.
   c. program.   d. CPU.

4. If you wanted to transfer information from one computer to another you might use a
   a. hard disk.   b. RAM chip.
   c. ROM chip.   d. diskette.

5. A group of computers connected by cables or telephone lines is a
   a. microprocessor.
   b. CPU.
   c. modem.
   d. network.

True or False

If the statement is true, write true. If it is false, change the underlined word or words to make the statement true.

6. A <u>transistor</u> changes alternating current into direct current.

7. Before semiconductors, electronic devices used <u>vacuum tubes</u> to control electric current.

8. A <u>microphone</u> is the part of a television that produces the image.

9. <u>Output</u> devices feed data into a computer.

10. The <u>Internet</u> can be described as a network of computer networks.

Checking Concepts

11. Compare an analog signal with a digital signal.

12. Define each of the following in your own words: diode, transistor, and integrated circuit.

13. Draw an illustration of an electromagnetic wave. Give three examples of electromagnetic waves.

14. Explain how a radio show is broadcast and received.

15. How does a cathode-ray tube create a picture?

16. How is the World Wide Web different from the Internet?

17. **Writing to Learn** Imagine that you have started your own small magazine. Choose a topic for your magazine, such as sports, fashion, science, or cooking. Then write three to four paragraphs describing how a computer and access to the Internet might help you.

Thinking Critically

18. **Comparing and Contrasting** What are some advantages of solid-state devices over vacuum tubes?

19. **Calculating** Each image on a television screen lasts for 1/30th of a second. How many images appear on the screen during a 30-minute program?

20. **Applying Concepts** A computer program is a list of instructions that tells a computer how to perform a task. Write a program that describes the steps involved in some task, such as walking your dog, taking out the trash, setting the table, or playing a game.

21. **Comparing and Contrasting** How do base-10 numbers and binary numbers differ? Explain how you read and write numbers in each system. Give examples.

22. **Making Judgments** Why does a government protect a computer program as the intellectual property of the author?

Applying Skills

Use the illustrations below to answer Questions 23–25.

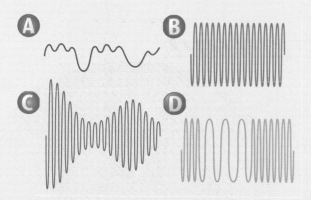

23. Predicting What would the audio signal in part A look like if it were converted to an AM radio signal? Draw a sketch to illustrate your answer.

24. Communicating What is represented in part B? Describe its basic characteristics.

25. Classifying Two radio transmitters send out electronic signals shown as part C and part D. How are the two forms alike and how are they different?

Performance **Assessment**

CHAPTER PROJECT 4

Project Wrap Up Present both the existing computer application and the new one you invented to the class. Provide diagrams of each and describe their operation. You might want to pretend you are trying to sell your new invention to the class. Prepare a poster describing the task that your new application will accomplish. Show yourself enjoying the benefits!

Reflect and Record In your journal, discuss what you've learned about computer applications. Think about the new computer application you developed. Is there a way to make it even better or more useful than you already have?

Test Preparation

Use these questions to prepare for standardized tests.

Read the passage. Then answer Questions 26–29.
José made a simple computer for a school science project. The only problem was that his computer could read and write only binary numbers. It did not translate to or from base-10 numbers. José asked the computer to add the following binary numbers:
`100 + 1111 + 110101`.

The computer's answer was 1001000.

26. What is the base number of the binary system?
 a. 1   **b.** 2
 c. 4   **d.** 8

27. What is each 1 or 0 in the binary system called?
 a. a bit   **b.** a byte
 c. a megabyte   **d.** a ram

28. Translate into the base-10 system the numbers José added.
 a. 100 + 1,111 + 110,101
 b. 2 + 2,222 + 220,202
 c. 4 + 15 + 53
 d. 6 + 20 + 30

29. Translate the computer's answer into the base-10 system.
 a. 42   **b.** 56
 c. 72   **d.** 1,001,000

E·D·I·S·O·N—
Genius of Invention

WHAT INVENTOR GAVE US

- *sound recording?*
- *motion pictures?*
- *electric lighting?*

Edison at his workbench

This scene shows New York City in 1881. An electric light high above Madison Square outshines the gas light in the foreground.

In 1881, the electric light in the picture at the left was a novelty. Streets and some homes were lit with gas, while other homes used oil lamps or candles. Thomas Edison was still developing his system of indoor electric lighting.

Electric lights brought with them a system of power distribution which made other uses of electricity possible. If you try to imagine living without any electrical appliances, you will understand the changes in everyday life that Edison started.

Thomas Edison (1847–1931) had almost no schooling. Yet his mind always bubbled with ideas. In addition to his lighting system, Edison invented the phonograph and the movie camera. He also made improvements to the telegraph and telephone. At the time of his death, Edison held 1,093 patents. A patent is a government license protecting an inventor's right to make and sell a product. One of Edison's most important ideas was never patented. He created the first laboratory for industrial research.

Edison's research laboratory in Menlo Park

The Wizard of Menlo Park

Before 1900 most inventors worked alone. Edison, in contrast, depended on a strong team of research co-workers to carry out his ideas. Edison had an unusual ability to inspire those who worked for him. A very hard worker himself, he demanded that everyone on his team also work long hours.

In 1870, he set up a workshop in Newark, New Jersey, to test new ideas and designs. Some of Edison's original team stayed with him for years. They included a Swiss clockmaker, an English engineer, and an American mechanic.

By 1876 Edison had enough money to set up an "invention factory." He chose the small town of Menlo Park, New Jersey. Menlo Park became the world's first industrial research laboratory. Soon a mathematician and a glass blower joined the team.

Edison's team often made improvements on other people's inventions. The light bulb is an example. Other scientists had invented electric lamps, but their light bulbs burned rapidly. The problem was to find a material for the filament that would not overheat or burn out quickly.

The Menlo Park team spent months testing hundreds of materials. First they rolled up each material into a long thin strand. Then they carbonized it, which meant baking it until it turned to charcoal. Then they tested it in a vacuum, or absence of air. Most materials failed in only a few minutes or a few hours. Edison tried platinum, a metallic element, with some success, but then went back to carbonized fibers. The team improved the vacuum inside the bulb. The glass blower tried differently shaped bulbs.

The breakthrough came in 1879. The first successful filament was a length of ordinary cotton thread, carefully carbonized. In December, the newspapers carried the headlines: "Success in a Cotton Thread" and "It Makes a Light, Without Gas or Flame."

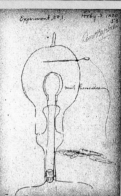

A light bulb is made of a wire, or filament, inside a glass bulb. Most of the air is removed from the bulb, making a vacuum. Electricity flowing through the wire makes it white hot, so that it glows. Edison's drawing of a light bulb is at the right.

Science Activity

Work together as a team to invent a new electrical device.

◆ What could a new electrical device help you do? How could it make your life easier?

◆ Brainstorm for possible products that would help you in some way. Write down all possible ideas.

◆ Evaluate each solution and agree on the best one.

◆ Plan your design and make a labeled drawing. List the supplies you will need. Note any new skills you should learn.

◆ Write down the steps you will use to build your device.

Lighting Manhattan

Edison recognized the value of publicity. Besides being a productive inventor, he knew how to promote himself. He made glowing predictions about his new electric system. Electricity would soon be so cheap, he said, that "only the rich would be able to afford candles."

Edison demonstrated his electric lights in spectacular displays at expositions in Paris and London. These displays led to his setting up companies in France, England, the Netherlands, and other parts of Europe.

When he built his first neighborhood generating station, Edison made a shrewd choice of location. The Pearl Street power station brought light and power to about 2.6 square kilometers of downtown Manhattan. It supplied businesses and factories as well as private homes. The circuits could light 400 light bulbs. Some of those lights were in the offices of J. P. Morgan, the leading banker and financier of the time. Others lights were located in the offices of *The New York Times.* Here's what the *Times* reporter wrote on September 5, 1882.

New York City—Broadway in the 1880s

The New York Times, September 5, 1882

"Yesterday for the first time The Times Building was illuminated by electricity. Mr. Edison had at last perfected his incandescent light, had put his machinery in order, and had started up his engines, and last evening his company lighted up about one-third of the lower City district in which The Times Building stands. . . .

It was not until about seven o'clock, when it began to grow dark, that the electric light really made itself known and showed how bright and steady it is. . . . It was a light that a man could sit down under and write for hours without the consciousness of having any artificial light about him. There was a very slight amount of heat from each lamp, but not nearly as much as from a gas-burner—one-fifteenth as much as from gas, the inventor says. The light was soft, mellow, and grateful to the eye, and it seemed almost like writing by daylight to have a light without a particle of flicker and with scarcely any heat to make the head ache. . . . The decision was unanimously in favor of the Edison electric lamp as against gas."

Language Arts Activity

The reporter who wrote the newspaper story observed details carefully and used them to write about an event—the first lights in his office. Look back at the story. Now write about the event as Edison would have told it to convince people to buy light bulbs and install electrical power systems. You could make an advertisement. Inform your readers about the product and persuade them to buy it.

Solving Practical Problems

As he grew older, Edison worried that American students were not learning mathematics well enough. To motivate students, he suggested using problems that related to real-life situations. In 1925, when he was 78, he proposed these problems as recorded in his notebooks. Note that light bulbs were called *lamps*. Tungsten is a metal used in light bulbs.

PROBLEM 1
"American power plants now serve 9,500,000 homes. The estimated number of homes in the United States is 21,000,000. What percentage receives electric power?"

PROBLEM 2
"It needs about 280,000,000 tungsten lamps [bulbs] each year to supply the market today. And yet the first lamp factory in the world—the Edison Lamp Works. . .—was not started until 1880, and I was told it would never pay. The output for our first year was about 25,000 globes [bulbs]. How many times that figure would be required for the present market?"

PROBLEM 3
"A household using 21 lamps requires about 7 new lamps each year. What percentage is this?"

Math Activity

Solve the four math problems that Edison wrote. To solve Problem 4, use 1902 prices. That year, incandescent light bulbs (or lamps) cost $ .30 each.

PROBLEM 4
"If these lamps had been bought at the retail prices of the first year of the lamp factory, they would have cost $1.25 each. How much would the family save by the decreased prices of today?"

Electrical Distribution

Electric lighting didn't begin with Edison's light bulb. Before the incandescent bulb, most electric lights were carbon arc lamps. An electric arc flashed between two carbon rods. Carbon arc lamps were used for public places such as railroad stations in both Europe and the United States. But they were too bright and too dangerous for most indoor uses.

Edison found a way to make indoor lighting practical. Along with the light bulb, he had to set up a system to distribute electricity to homes and business. That system included generators, underground cables, junction boxes, and meters.

Local power companies grew slowly. Laying cables to carry power was slow and expensive. In the 1920s, less than half the homes in cities had electricity. And less than 10 percent of rural areas had electricity. Only in 1935 was a program begun to bring power to the countryside.

Social Studies Activity

Look at the recent satellite photo of the United States at night. It shows how electric lights now light up the country from coast to coast. Using a map of the United States, identify the regions that are the brightest. What cities are located there? Which states have the most urban areas? Which have the least? Use an almanac to find out the population of 5 of the largest cities. Compare these data with the total United States population.

History of the phonograph

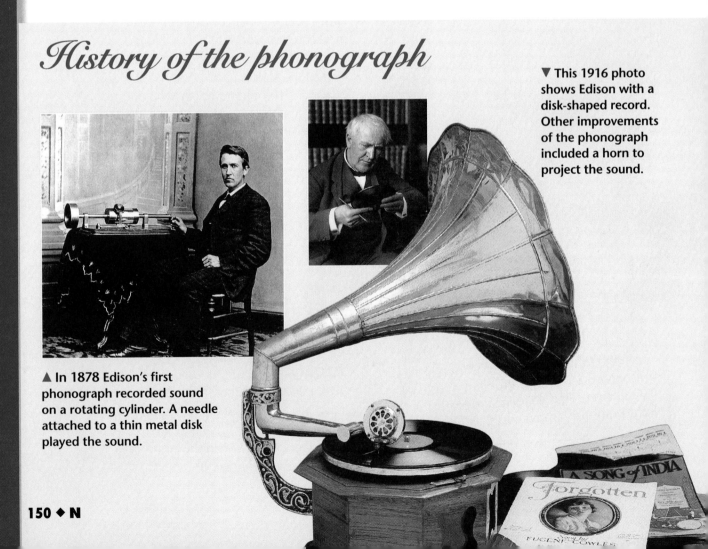

▼ This 1916 photo shows Edison with a disk-shaped record. Other improvements of the phonograph included a horn to project the sound.

▲ In 1878 Edison's first phonograph recorded sound on a rotating cylinder. A needle attached to a thin metal disk played the sound.

A SONG of INDIA

Forgotten

As this satellite image shows, the glow of street lights is visible from space.

Modern Times

Many of the inventions that came out of Menlo Park still affect things we do today. Work in pairs to research one of Edison's inventions. Or research another scientist's inventions. Find out how the device changed and improved in the 1900s. Write up your research and present it to the class. If the device is no longer used, explain what has replaced it. Here are a few inventions from which to choose. (Not all of them were Edison's.)

- stock ticker
- telegraph
- phonograph
- disk record
- voting machine
- electric pen and press
- typewriter
- telephone
- automobile
- radio transmitter
- vacuum tube
- mechanical music
- linotype

By the 1950s, phonographs used electric motors and electronic amplifiers. The quality of sound was better, and the volume could be much greater.

▼ 78 rpm record

◀ 45 rpm records

▲ 33⅓ rpm record

Records played longer as the standard playing speed was reduced from 78 revolutions per minute to 45 and $33\frac{1}{3}$ revolutions per minute.

Compact discs have recordings on them, and they are shaped like phonograph records. But are they related to Edison's invention?

Think Like a Scientist

Although you may not know it, you think like a scientist every day. Whenever you ask a question and explore possible answers, you use many of the same skills that scientists do. Some of these skills are described on this page.

Observing

When you use one or more of your five senses to gather information about the world, you are **observing.** Hearing a dog bark, counting twelve green seeds, and smelling smoke are all observations. To increase the power of their senses, scientists sometimes use microscopes, telescopes, or other instruments that help them make more detailed observations.

An observation must be an accurate report of what your senses detect. It is important to keep careful records of your observations in science class by writing or drawing in a notebook. The information collected through observations is called evidence, or data.

Inferring

When you interpret an observation, you are **inferring,** or making an inference. For example, if you hear your dog barking, you may infer that someone is at your front door. To make this inference, you combine the evidence—the barking dog—and your experience or knowledge—you know that your dog barks when strangers approach—to reach a logical conclusion.

Notice that an inference is not a fact; it is only one of many possible interpretations for an observation. For example, your dog may be barking because it wants to go for a walk. An inference may turn out to be incorrect even if it is based on accurate observations and logical reasoning. The only way to find out if an inference is correct is to investigate further.

Predicting

When you listen to the weather forecast, you hear many predictions about the next day's weather—what the temperature will be, whether it will rain, and how windy it will be. Weather forecasters use observations and knowledge of weather patterns to predict the weather. The skill of **predicting** involves making an inference about a future event based on current evidence or past experience.

Because a prediction is an inference, it may prove to be false. In science class, you can test some of your predictions by doing experiments. For example, suppose you predict that larger paper airplanes can fly farther than smaller airplanes. How could you test your prediction?

ACTIVITY Use the photograph to answer the questions below.

Observing Look closely at the photograph. List at least three observations.

Inferring Use your observations to make an inference about what has happened. What experience or knowledge did you use to make the inference?

Predicting Predict what will happen next. On what evidence or experience do you base your prediction?

Classifying

Could you imagine searching for a book in the library if the books were shelved in no particular order? Your trip to the library would be an all-day event! Luckily, librarians group together books on similar topics or by the same author. Grouping together items that are alike in some way is called **classifying.** You can classify items in many ways: by size, by shape, by use, and by other important characteristics.

Like librarians, scientists use the skill of classifying to organize information and objects. When things are sorted into groups, the relationships among them become easier to understand.

ACTIVITY

Classify the objects in the photograph into two groups based on any characteristic you choose. Then use another characteristic to classify the objects into three groups.

Making Models

Have you ever drawn a picture to help someone understand what you were saying? Such a drawing is one type of model. A model is a picture, diagram, computer image, or other representation of a complex object or process. **Making models** helps people understand things that they cannot observe directly.

Scientists often use models to represent things that are either very large or very small, such as the planets in the solar system, or the parts of a cell. Such models are physical models—drawings or three-dimensional structures that look like the real thing. Other models are mental models— mathematical equations or words that describe how something works.

ACTIVITY

This student is using a model to demonstrate what causes day and night on Earth. What do the flashlight and the tennis ball in the model represent?

Communicating

Whenever you talk on the phone, write a letter, or listen to your teacher at school, you are communicating. **Communicating** is the process of sharing ideas and information with other people. Communicating effectively requires many skills, including writing, reading, speaking, listening, and making models.

Scientists communicate to share results, information, and opinions. Scientists often communicate about their work in journals, over the telephone, in

letters, and on the Internet. They also attend scientific meetings where they share their ideas with one another in person.

ACTIVITY

On a sheet of paper, write out clear, detailed directions for tying your shoe. Then exchange directions with a partner. Follow your partner's directions exactly. How successful were you at tying your shoe? How could your partner have communicated more clearly?

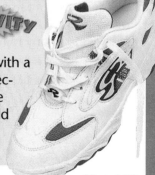

Making Measurements

When scientists make observations, it is not sufficient to say that something is "big" or "heavy." Instead, scientists use instruments to measure just how big or heavy an object is. By measuring, scientists can express their observations more precisely and communicate more information about what they observe.

Measuring in SI

The standard system of measurement used by scientists around the world is known as the International System of Units, which is abbreviated as SI (in French, *Système International d'Unités*). SI units are easy to use because they are based on multiples of 10. Each unit is ten times larger than the next smallest unit and one tenth the size of the next largest unit. The table lists the prefixes used to name the most common SI units.

Common SI Prefixes

Prefix	Symbol	Meaning
kilo-	k	1,000
hecto-	h	100
deka-	da	10
deci-	d	0.1 (one tenth)
centi-	c	0.01 (one hundredth)
milli-	m	0.001 (one thousandth)

Length To measure length, or the distance between two points, the unit of measure is the **meter (m).** The distance from the floor to a doorknob is approximately one meter. Long distances, such as the distance between two cities, are measured in kilometers (km). Small lengths are measured in centimeters (cm) or millimeters (mm). Scientists use metric rulers and meter sticks to measure length.

Common Conversions

1 km = 1,000 m
1 m = 100 cm
1 m = 1,000 mm
1 cm = 10 mm

Liquid Volume To measure the volume of a liquid, or the amount of space it takes up, you will use a unit of measure known as the **liter (L).** One liter is the approximate volume of a medium-size carton of milk. Smaller volumes are measured in milliliters (mL). Scientists use graduated cylinders to measure liquid volume.

Common Conversion

1 L = 1,000 mL

ACTIVITY

The larger lines on the metric ruler in the picture show centimeter divisions, while the smaller, unnumbered lines show millimeter divisions. How many centimeters long is the shell? How many millimeters long is it?

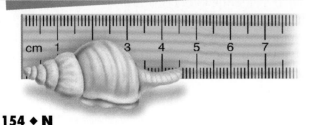

ACTIVITY

The graduated cylinder in the picture is marked in milliliter divisions. Notice that the water in the cylinder has a curved surface. This curved surface is called the *meniscus.* To measure the volume, you must read the level at the lowest point of the meniscus. What is the volume of water in this graduated cylinder?

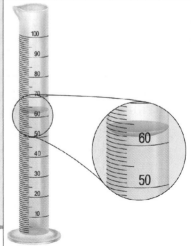

Mass To measure mass, or the amount of matter in an object, you will use a unit of measure known as the **gram (g)**. One gram is approximately the mass of a paper clip. Larger masses are measured in kilograms (kg). Scientists use a balance to find the mass of an object.

Common Conversion

1 kg = 1,000 g

The mass of the apple in the picture is measured in kilograms. What is the mass of the apple? Suppose a recipe for applesauce called for one kilogram of apples. About how many apples would you need?

ACTIVITY

Temperature
To measure the temperature of a substance, you will use the **Celsius scale**. Temperature is measured in degrees Celsius (°C) using a Celsius thermometer. Water freezes at 0°C and boils at 100°C.

ACTIVITY

What is the temperature of the liquid in degrees Celsius?

Converting SI Units

To use the SI system, you must know how to convert between units. Converting from one unit to another involves the skill of **calculating**, or using mathematical operations. Converting between SI units is similar to converting between dollars and dimes because both systems are based on multiples of ten.

Suppose you want to convert a length of 80 centimeters to meters. Follow these steps to convert between units.

1. Begin by writing down the measurement you want to convert—in this example, 80 centimeters.
2. Write a conversion factor that represents the relationship between the two units you are converting. In this example, the relationship is *1 meter = 100 centimeters.* Write this conversion factor as a fraction, making sure to place the units you are converting from (centimeters, in this example) in the denominator.

3. Multiply the measurement you want to convert by the fraction. When you do this, the units in the first measurement will cancel out with the units in the denominator. Your answer will be in the units you are converting to (meters, in this example).

Example

80 centimeters = ____?____ meters

$$80 \text{ centimeters} \times \frac{1 \text{ meter}}{100 \text{ centimeters}} = \frac{80 \text{ meters}}{100}$$

$$= 0.8 \text{ meters}$$

Convert between the following units.

ACTIVITY

1. 600 millimeters = _?_ meters
2. 0.35 liters = _?_ milliliters
3. 1,050 grams = _?_ kilograms

N ◆ 155

Conducting a Scientific Investigation

In some ways, scientists are like detectives, piecing together clues to learn about a process or event. One way that scientists gather clues is by carrying out experiments. An experiment tests an idea in a careful, orderly manner. Although experiments do not all follow the same steps in the same order, many follow a pattern similar to the one described here.

Posing Questions

Experiments begin by asking a scientific question. A scientific question is one that can be answered by gathering evidence. For example, the question "Which freezes faster—fresh water or salt water?" is a scientific question because you can carry out an investigation and gather information to answer the question.

Developing a Hypothesis

The next step is to form a hypothesis. A **hypothesis** is a possible explanation for a set of observations or answer to a scientific question. In science, a hypothesis must be something that can be tested. A hypothesis can be worded as an *If…then…*statement. For example, a hypothesis might be *"If I add salt to fresh water, then the water will take longer to freeze."* A hypothesis worded this way serves as a rough outline of the experiment you should perform.

Designing an Experiment

Next you need to plan a way to test your hypothesis. Your plan should be written out as a step-by-step procedure and should describe the observations or measurements you will make.

Two important steps involved in designing an experiment are controlling variables and forming operational definitions.

Controlling Variables In a well-designed experiment, you need to keep all variables the same except for one. A **variable** is any factor that can change in an experiment. The factor that you change is called the **manipulated variable.** In this experiment, the manipulated variable is the amount of salt added to the water. Other factors, such as the amount of water or the starting temperature, are kept constant.

The factor that changes as a result of the manipulated variable is called the responding variable. The **responding variable** is what you measure or observe to obtain your results. In this experiment, the responding variable is how long the water takes to freeze.

An experiment in which all factors except one are kept constant is a **controlled experiment.** Most controlled experiments include a test called the control. In this experiment, Container 3 is the control. Because no salt is added to Container 3, you can compare the results from the other containers to it. Any difference in results must be due to the addition of salt alone.

Forming Operational Definitions
Another important aspect of a well-designed experiment is having clear operational definitions. An **operational definition** is a statement that describes how a particular variable is to be measured or how a term is to be defined. For example, in this experiment, how will you determine if the water has frozen? You might decide to insert a stick in each container at the start of the experiment. Your operational definition of "frozen" would be the time at which the stick can no longer move.

EXPERIMENTAL PROCEDURE

1. Fill 3 containers with 300 milliliters of cold tap water.

2. Add 10 grams of salt to Container 1; stir. Add 20 grams of salt to Container 2; stir. Add no salt to Container 3.

3. Place the 3 containers in a freezer.

4. Check the containers every 15 minutes. Record your observations.

Interpreting Data

The observations and measurements you make in an experiment are called data. At the end of an experiment, you need to analyze the data to look for any patterns or trends. Patterns often become clear if you organize your data in a data table or graph. Then think through what the data reveal. Do they support your hypothesis? Do they point out a flaw in your experiment? Do you need to collect more data?

Drawing Conclusions

A conclusion is a statement that sums up what you have learned from an experiment. When you draw a conclusion, you need to decide whether the data you collected support your hypothesis or not. You may need to repeat an experiment several times before you can draw any conclusions from it. Conclusions often lead you to pose new questions and plan new experiments to answer them.

Is a ball's bounce affected by the height from which it is dropped? Using the steps just described, plan a controlled experiment to investigate this problem. **ACTIVITY**

Thinking Critically

Has a friend ever asked for your advice about a problem? If so, you may have helped your friend think through the problem in a logical way. Without knowing it, you used critical-thinking skills to help your friend. Critical thinking involves the use of reasoning and logic to solve problems or make decisions. Some critical-thinking skills are described below.

Comparing and Contrasting

When you examine two objects for similarities and differences, you are using the skill of **comparing and contrasting.** Comparing involves identifying similarities, or common characteristics. Contrasting involves identifying differences. Analyzing objects in this way can help you discover details that you might otherwise overlook.

ACTIVITY

Compare and contrast the two animals in the photo. First list all the similarities that you see. Then list all the differences.

Applying Concepts

When you use your knowledge about one situation to make sense of a similar situation, you are using the skill of **applying concepts.** Being able to transfer your knowledge from one situation to another shows that you truly understand a concept. You may use this skill in answering test questions that present different problems from the ones you've reviewed in class.

ACTIVITY

You have just learned that water takes longer to freeze when other substances are mixed into it. Use this knowledge to explain why people need a substance called antifreeze in their car's radiator in the winter.

Interpreting Illustrations

Diagrams, photographs, and maps are included in textbooks to help clarify what you read. These illustrations show processes, places, and ideas in a visual manner. The skill called **interpreting illustrations** can help you learn from these visual elements. To understand an illustration, take the time to study the illustration along with all the written information that accompanies it. Captions identify the key concepts shown in the illustration. Labels point out the important parts of a diagram or map, while keys identify the symbols used in a map.

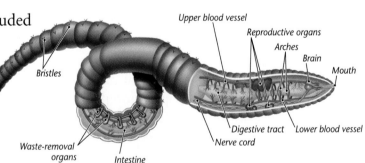

Upper blood vessel
Reproductive organs
Arches
Brain
Mouth
Bristles
Digestive tract
Lower blood vessel
Nerve cord
Waste-removal organs
Intestine

▲ **Internal anatomy of an earthworm**

ACTIVITY

Study the diagram above. Then write a short paragraph explaining what you have learned.

Relating Cause and Effect

If one event causes another event to occur, the two events are said to have a cause-and-effect relationship. When you determine that such a relationship exists between two events, you use a skill called **relating cause and effect.** For example, if you notice an itchy, red bump on your skin, you might infer that a mosquito bit you. The mosquito bite is the cause, and the bump is the effect.

It is important to note that two events do not necessarily have a cause-and-effect relationship just because they occur together. Scientists carry out experiments or use past experience to determine whether a cause-and-effect relationship exists.

ACTIVITY

You are on a camping trip and your flashlight has stopped working. List some possible causes for the flashlight malfunction. How could you determine which cause-and-effect relationship has left you in the dark?

Making Generalizations

When you draw a conclusion about an entire group based on information about only some of the group's members, you are using a skill called **making generalizations.** For a generalization to be valid, the sample you choose must be large enough and representative of the entire group. You might, for example, put this skill to work at a farm stand if you see a sign that says, "Sample some grapes before you buy." If you sample a few sweet grapes, you may conclude that all the grapes are sweet—and purchase a large bunch.

ACTIVITY

A team of scientists needs to determine whether the water in a large reservoir is safe to drink. How could they use the skill of making generalizations to help them? What should they do?

Making Judgments

When you evaluate something to decide whether it is good or bad, or right or wrong, you are using a skill called **making judgments.** For example, you make judgments when you decide to eat healthful foods or to pick up litter in a park. Before you make a judgment, you need to think through the pros and cons of a situation, and identify the values or standards that you hold.

ACTIVITY

Should children and teens be required to wear helmets when bicycling? Explain why you feel the way you do.

Problem Solving

When you use critical-thinking skills to resolve an issue or decide on a course of action, you are using a skill called **problem solving.** Some problems, such as how to convert a fraction into a decimal, are straightforward. Other problems, such as figuring out why your computer has stopped working, are complex. Some complex problems can be solved using the trial and error method—try out one solution first, and if that doesn't work, try another. Other useful problem-solving strategies include making models and brainstorming possible solutions with a partner.

Organizing Information

As you read this textbook, how can you make sense of all the information it contains? Some useful tools to help you organize information are shown on this page. These tools are called *graphic organizers* because they give you a visual picture of a topic, showing at a glance how key concepts are related.

Concept Maps

Concept maps are useful tools for organizing information on broad topics. A concept map begins with a general concept and shows how it can be broken down into more specific concepts. In that way, relationships between concepts become easier to understand.

A concept map is constructed by placing concept words (usually nouns) in ovals and connecting them with linking words. Often, the most general concept word is placed at the top, and the words become more specific as you move downward. Often the linking words, which are written on a line extending between two ovals, describe the relationship between the two concepts they connect. If you follow any string of concepts and linking words down the map, it should read like a sentence.

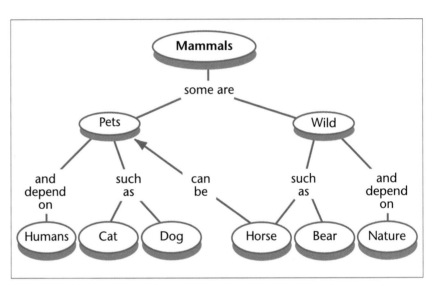

Some concept maps include linking words that connect a concept on one branch of the map to a concept on another branch. These linking words, called cross-linkages, show more complex interrelationships among concepts.

Compare/Contrast Tables

Compare/contrast tables are useful tools for sorting out the similarities and differences between two or more items. A table provides an organized framework in which to compare items based on specific characteristics that you identify.

To create a compare/contrast table, list the items to be compared across the top of a table. Then list the characteristics that will form the basis of your comparison in the left-hand column. Complete the table by filling in information about each characteristic, first for one item and then for the other.

Characteristic	Baseball	Basketball
Number of Players	9	5
Playing Field	Baseball diamond	Basketball court
Equipment	Bat, baseball, mitts	Basket, basketball

Venn Diagrams

Another way to show similarities and differences between items is with a Venn diagram. A Venn diagram consists of two or more circles that partially overlap. Each circle represents a particular concept or idea. Common characteristics, or similarities, are written within the area of overlap between the two circles. Unique characteristics, or differences, are written in the parts of the circles outside the area of overlap.

To create a Venn diagram, draw two overlapping circles. Label the circles with the names of the items being compared. Write the unique characteristics in each circle outside the area of overlap. Then write the shared characteristics within the area of overlap.

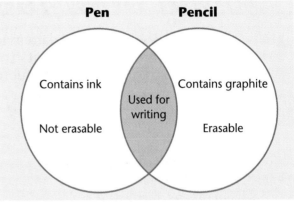

Flowcharts

A flowchart can help you understand the order in which certain events have occurred or should occur. Flowcharts are useful for outlining the stages in a process or the steps in a procedure.

To make a flowchart, write a brief description of each event in a box. Place the first event at the top of the page, followed by the second event, the third event, and so on. Then draw an arrow to connect each event to the one that occurs next.

Preparing Pasta

Boil water

↓

Cook pasta

↓

Drain water

↓

Add sauce

Cycle Diagrams

A cycle diagram can be used to show a sequence of events that is continuous, or cyclical. A continuous sequence does not have an end because, when the final event is over, the first event begins again. Like a flowchart, a cycle diagram can help you understand the order of events.

To create a cycle diagram, write a brief description of each event in a box. Place one event at the top of the page in the center. Then, moving in a clockwise direction around an imaginary circle, write each event in its proper sequence. Draw arrows that connect each event to the one that occurs next, forming a continuous circle.

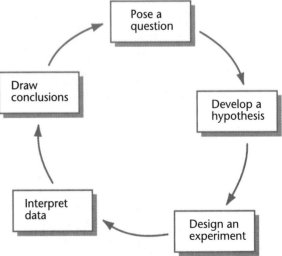

Steps in a Science Experiment

Creating Data Tables and Graphs

How can you make sense of the data in a science experiment? The first step is to organize the data to help you understand them. Data tables and graphs are helpful tools for organizing data.

Data Tables

You have gathered your materials and set up your experiment. But before you start, you need to plan a way to record what happens during the experiment. By creating a data table, you can record your observations and measurements in an orderly way.

Suppose, for example, that a scientist conducted an experiment to find out how many Calories people of different body masses burn while doing various activities. The data table shows the results.

Notice in this data table that the manipulated variable (body mass) is the heading of one column. The responding

CALORIES BURNED IN 30 MINUTES OF ACTIVITY			
Body Mass	Experiment 1 Bicycling	Experiment 2 Playing Basketball	Experiment 3 Watching Television
30 kg	60 Calories	120 Calories	21 Calories
40 kg	77 Calories	164 Calories	27 Calories
50 kg	95 Calories	206 Calories	33 Calories
60 kg	114 Calories	248 Calories	38 Calories

variable (for Experiment 1, the number of Calories burned while bicycling) is the heading of the next column. Additional columns were added for related experiments.

Bar Graphs

To compare how many Calories a person burns doing various activities, you could create a bar graph. A bar graph is used to display data in a number of separate, or distinct, categories. In this example, bicycling, playing basketball, and watching television are three separate categories.

To create a bar graph, follow these steps.

1. On graph paper, draw a horizontal, or *x*-, axis and a vertical, or *y*-, axis.
2. Write the names of the categories to be graphed along the horizontal axis. Include an overall label for the axis as well.
3. Label the vertical axis with the name of the responding variable. Include units of measurement. Then create a scale along the axis by marking off equally spaced numbers that cover the range of the data collected.
4. For each category, draw a solid bar using the scale on the vertical axis to determine the

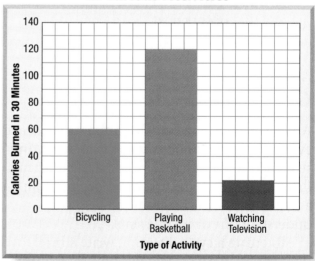

Calories Burned by a 30-kilogram Person in Various Activities

appropriate height. For example, for bicycling, draw the bar as high as the 60 mark on the vertical axis. Make all the bars the same width and leave equal spaces between them.

5. Add a title that describes the graph.

Line Graphs

To see whether a relationship exists between body mass and the number of Calories burned while bicycling, you could create a line graph. A line graph is used to display data that show how one variable (the responding variable) changes in response to another variable (the manipulated variable). You can use a line graph when your manipulated variable is *continuous*, that is, when there are other points between the ones that you tested. In this example, body mass is a continuous variable because there are other body masses between 30 and 40 kilograms (for example, 31 kilograms). Time is another example of a continuous variable.

Line graphs are powerful tools because they allow you to estimate values for conditions that you did not test in the experiment. For example, you can use the line graph to estimate that a 35-kilogram person would burn 68 Calories while bicycling.

To create a line graph, follow these steps.

1. On graph paper, draw a horizontal, or *x*-, axis and a vertical, or *y*-, axis.
2. Label the horizontal axis with the name of the manipulated variable. Label the vertical axis with the name of the responding variable. Include units of measurement.
3. Create a scale on each axis by marking off equally spaced numbers that cover the range of the data collected.
4. Plot a point on the graph for each piece of data. In the line graph above, the dotted lines show how to plot the first data point (30 kilograms and 60 Calories). Draw an imaginary vertical line extending up from the horizontal axis at the 30-kilogram mark. Then draw an imaginary horizontal line extending across from the vertical axis at the 60-Calorie mark. Plot the point where the two lines intersect.

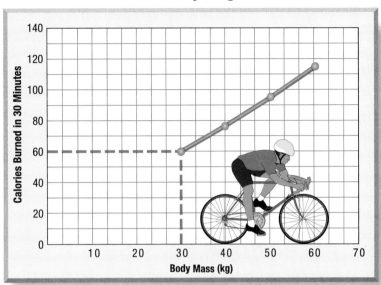

Effect of Body Mass on Calories Burned While Bicycling

5. Connect the plotted points with a solid line. (In some cases, it may be more appropriate to draw a line that shows the general trend of the plotted points. In those cases, some of the points may fall above or below the line. Also, not all graphs are linear. It may be more appropriate to draw a curve to connect the points.)
6. Add a title that identifies the variables or relationship in the graph.

> Create line graphs to display the data from Experiment 2 and Experiment 3 in the data table.
>
> **ACTIVITY**

> You read in the newspaper that a total of 4 centimeters of rain fell in your area in June, 2.5 centimeters fell in July, and 1.5 centimeters fell in August. What type of graph would you use to display these data? Use graph paper to create the graph.
>
> **ACTIVITY**

Circle Graphs

Like bar graphs, circle graphs can be used to display data in a number of separate categories. Unlike bar graphs, however, circle graphs can only be used when you have data for *all* the categories that make up a given topic. A circle graph is sometimes called a pie chart because it resembles a pie cut into slices. The pie represents the entire topic, while the slices represent the individual categories. The size of a slice indicates what percentage of the whole a particular category makes up.

The data table below shows the results of a survey in which 24 teenagers were asked to identify their favorite sport. The data were then used to create the circle graph at the right.

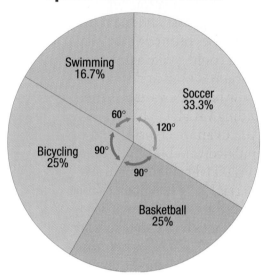

Sports That Teens Prefer

FAVORITE SPORTS	
Sport	Number of Students
Soccer	8
Basketball	6
Bicycling	6
Swimming	4

To create a circle graph, follow these steps.

1. Use a compass to draw a circle. Mark the center of the circle with a point. Then draw a line from the center point to the top of the circle.
2. Determine the size of each "slice" by setting up a proportion where *x* equals the number of degrees in a slice. (NOTE: A circle contains 360 degrees.) For example, to find the number of degrees in the "soccer" slice, set up the following proportion:

$$\frac{\text{students who prefer soccer}}{\text{total number of students}} = \frac{x}{\text{total number of degrees in a circle}}$$

$$\frac{8}{24} = \frac{x}{360}$$

Cross-multiply and solve for *x*.

$$24x = 8 \times 360$$
$$x = 120$$

The "soccer" slice should contain 120 degrees.

3. Use a protractor to measure the angle of the first slice, using the line you drew to the top of the circle as the 0° line. Draw a line from the center of the circle to the edge for the angle you measured.
4. Continue around the circle by measuring the size of each slice with the protractor. Start measuring from the edge of the previous slice so the wedges do not overlap. When you are done, the entire circle should be filled in.
5. Determine the percentage of the whole circle that each slice represents. To do this, divide the number of degrees in a slice by the total number of degrees in a circle (360), and multiply by 100%. For the "soccer" slice, you can find the percentage as follows:

$$\frac{120}{360} \times 100\% = 33.3\%$$

6. Use a different color to shade in each slice. Label each slice with the name of the category and with the percentage of the whole it represents.
7. Add a title to the circle graph.

ACTIVITY

In a class of 28 students, 12 students take the bus to school, 10 students walk, and 6 students ride their bicycles. Create a circle graph to display these data.

Laboratory Safety

Safety Symbols

These symbols alert you to possible dangers in the laboratory and remind you to work carefully.

Safety Goggles Always wear safety goggles to protect your eyes in any activity involving chemicals, flames or heating, or the possibility of broken glassware.

Lab Apron Wear a laboratory apron to protect your skin and clothing from damage.

Breakage You are working with materials that may be breakable, such as glass containers, glass tubing, thermometers, or funnels. Handle breakable materials with care. Do not touch broken glassware.

Heat-resistant Gloves Use an oven mitt or other hand protection when handling hot materials. Hot plates, hot glassware, or hot water can cause burns. Do not touch hot objects with your bare hands.

Heating Use a clamp or tongs to pick up hot glassware. Do not touch hot objects with your bare hands.

Sharp Object Pointed-tip scissors, scalpels, knives, needles, pins, or tacks are sharp. They can cut or puncture your skin. Always direct a sharp edge or point away from yourself and others. Use sharp instruments only as instructed.

Electric Shock Avoid the possibility of electric shock. Never use electrical equipment around water, or when the equipment is wet or your hands are wet. Be sure cords are untangled and cannot trip anyone. Disconnect the equipment when it is not in use.

Corrosive Chemical You are working with an acid or another corrosive chemical. Avoid getting it on your skin or clothing, or in your eyes. Do not inhale the vapors. Wash your hands when you are finished with the activity.

Poison Do not let any poisonous chemical come in contact with your skin, and do not inhale its vapors. Wash your hands when you are finished with the activity.

Physical Safety When an experiment involves physical activity, take precautions to avoid injuring yourself or others. Follow instructions from your teacher. Alert your teacher if there is any reason you should not participate in the activity.

Animal Safety Treat live animals with care to avoid harming the animals or yourself. Working with animal parts or preserved animals also may require caution. Wash your hands when you are finished with the activity.

Plant Safety Handle plants in the laboratory or during field work only as directed by your teacher. If you are allergic to certain plants, tell your teacher before doing an activity in which those plants are used. Avoid touching harmful plants such as poison ivy, poison oak, or poison sumac, or plants with thorns. Wash your hands when you are finished with the activity.

Flames You may be working with flames from a lab burner, candle, or matches. Tie back loose hair and clothing. Follow instructions from your teacher about lighting and extinguishing flames.

No Flames Flammable materials may be present. Make sure there are no flames, sparks, or other exposed heat sources present.

Fumes When poisonous or unpleasant vapors may be involved, work in a ventilated area. Avoid inhaling vapors directly. Only test an odor when directed to do so by your teacher, and use a wafting motion to direct the vapor toward your nose.

Disposal Chemicals and other laboratory materials used in the activity must be disposed of safely. Follow the instructions from your teacher.

Hand Washing Wash your hands thoroughly when finished with the activity. Use antibacterial soap and warm water. Lather both sides of your hands and between your fingers. Rinse well.

General Safety Awareness You may see this symbol when none of the symbols described earlier appears. In this case, follow the specific instructions provided. You may also see this symbol when you are asked to develop your own procedure in a lab. Have your teacher approve your plan before you go further.

Science Safety Rules

To prepare yourself to work safely in the laboratory, read over the following safety rules. Then read them a second time. Make sure you understand and follow each rule. Ask your teacher to explain any rules you do not understand.

Dress Code

1. To protect yourself from injuring your eyes, wear safety goggles whenever you work with chemicals, burners, glassware, or any substance that might get into your eyes. If you wear contact lenses, notify your teacher.
2. Wear a lab apron or coat whenever you work with corrosive chemicals or substances that can stain.
3. Tie back long hair to keep it away from any chemicals, flames, or equipment.
4. Remove or tie back any article of clothing or jewelry that can hang down and touch chemicals, flames, or equipment. Roll up or secure long sleeves.
5. Never wear open shoes or sandals.

General Precautions

6. Read all directions for an experiment several times before beginning the activity. Carefully follow all written and oral instructions. If you are in doubt about any part of the experiment, ask your teacher for assistance.
7. Never perform activities that are not assigned or authorized by your teacher. Obtain permission before "experimenting" on your own. Never handle any equipment unless you have specific permission.
8. Never perform lab activities without direct supervision.
9. Never eat or drink in the laboratory.
10. Keep work areas clean and tidy at all times. Bring only notebooks and lab manuals or written lab procedures to the work area. All other items, such as purses and backpacks, should be left in a designated area.
11. Do not engage in horseplay.

First Aid

12. Always report all accidents or injuries to your teacher, no matter how minor. Notify your teacher immediately about any fires.
13. Learn what to do in case of specific accidents, such as getting acid in your eyes or on your skin. (Rinse acids from your body with lots of water.)
14. Be aware of the location of the first-aid kit, but do not use it unless instructed by your teacher. In case of injury, your teacher should administer first aid. Your teacher may also send you to the school nurse or call a physician.
15. Know the location of emergency equipment, such as the fire extinguisher and fire blanket, and know how to use it.
16. Know the location of the nearest telephone and whom to contact in an emergency.

Heating and Fire Safety

17. Never use a heat source, such as a candle, burner, or hot plate, without wearing safety goggles.
18. Never heat anything unless instructed to do so. A chemical that is harmless when cool may be dangerous when heated.
19. Keep all combustible materials away from flames. Never use a flame or spark near a combustible chemical.
20. Never reach across a flame.
21. Before using a laboratory burner, make sure you know proper procedures for lighting and adjusting the burner, as demonstrated by your teacher. Do not touch the burner. It may be hot. And never leave a lighted burner unattended!
22. Chemicals can splash or boil out of a heated test tube. When heating a substance in a test tube, make sure that the mouth of the tube is not pointed at you or anyone else.
23. Never heat a liquid in a closed container. The expanding gases produced may blow the container apart.
24. Before picking up a container that has been heated, hold the back of your hand near it. If you can feel heat on the back of your hand, the container is too hot to handle. Use an oven mitt to pick up a container that has been heated.

Using Chemicals Safely

25. Never mix chemicals "for the fun of it." You might produce a dangerous, possibly explosive substance.

26. Never put your face near the mouth of a container that holds chemicals. Many chemicals are poisonous. Never touch, taste, or smell a chemical unless you are instructed by your teacher to do so.

27. Use only those chemicals needed in the activity. Read and double-check labels on supply bottles before removing any chemicals. Take only as much as you need. Keep all containers closed when chemicals are not being used.

28. Dispose of all chemicals as instructed by your teacher. To avoid contamination, never return chemicals to their original containers. Never simply pour chemicals or other substances into the sink or trash containers.

29. Be extra careful when working with acids or bases. Pour all chemicals over the sink or a container, not over your work surface.

30. If you are instructed to test for odors, use a wafting motion to direct the odors to your nose. Do not inhale the fumes directly from the container.

31. When mixing an acid and water, always pour the water into the container first and then add the acid to the water. Never pour water into an acid.

32. Take extreme care not to spill any material in the laboratory. Wash chemical spills and splashes immediately with plenty of water. Immediately begin rinsing with water any acids that get on your skin or clothing, and notify your teacher of any acid spill at the same time.

Using Glassware Safely

33. Never force glass tubing or thermometers into a rubber stopper or rubber tubing. Have your teacher insert the glass tubing or thermometer if required for an activity.

34. If you are using a laboratory burner, use a wire screen to protect glassware from any flame. Never heat glassware that is not thoroughly dry on the outside.

35. Keep in mind that hot glassware looks cool. Never pick up glassware without first checking to see if it is hot. Use an oven mitt. See rule 24.

36. Never use broken or chipped glassware. If glassware breaks, notify your teacher and dispose of the glass-ware in the proper broken-glassware container. Never handle broken glass with your bare hands.

37. Never eat or drink from lab glassware.

38. Thoroughly clean glassware before putting it away.

Using Sharp Instruments

39. Handle scalpels or other sharp instruments with extreme care. Never cut material toward you; cut away from you.

40. Immediately notify your teacher if you cut your skin when working in the laboratory.

Animal and Plant Safety

41. Never perform experiments that cause pain, discomfort, or harm to animals. This rule applies at home as well as in the classroom.

42. Animals should be handled only if absolutely necessary. Your teacher will instruct you as to how to handle each animal species brought into the classroom.

43. If you know that you are allergic to certain plants, molds, or animals, tell your teacher before doing an activity in which these are used.

44. During field work, protect your skin by wearing long pants, long sleeves, socks, and closed shoes. Know how to recognize the poisonous plants and fungi in your area, as well as plants with thorns, and avoid contact with them. Never eat any part of a plant or fungus.

45. Wash your hands thoroughly after handling animals or a cage containing animals. Wash your hands when you are finished with any activity involving animal parts, plants, or soil.

End-of-Experiment Rules

46. After an experiment has been completed, turn off all burners or hot plates. If you used a gas burner, check that the gas-line valve to the burner is off. Unplug hot plates.

47. Turn off and unplug any other electrical equipment that you used.

48. Clean up your work area and return all equipment to its proper place.

49. Dispose of waste materials as instructed by your teacher.

50. Wash your hands after every experiment.

Glossary

alternating current Current consisting of charges that move back and forth in a circuit. (p. 86)

ammeter A device used to measure current in a circuit. (p. 60)

amplitude The height of a wave from the center to a crest or trough. (p. 124)

amplitude modulation (AM) Changes the amplitude of the carrier wave to match the amplitude of the signal. (p. 124)

analog signal An electric current that is varied smoothly to represent information. (p. 113)

armature The moving part of an electric motor, consisting of dozens or hundreds of loops of wire wrapped around an iron core. (p. 81)

atom The smallest particle of an element that has the properties of that element. (p. 18)

aurora A glowing region produced by the interaction of charged particles from the sun and atoms in the atmosphere. (p. 28)

battery A combination of two or more electrochemical cells in series. (p. 102)

binary system A number system using combinations of only two digits, 0 and 1; used by computers. (p. 128)

bit Each binary digit, 1 or 0, in the binary system. (p. 129)

brushes The contact points connected to a current source and the commutator of a motor. (p. 81)

byte Arrangement of 8 bits. (p. 129)

cathode-ray tube (CRT) A sealed glass vacuum tube that uses electrons to produce images on a screen; picture tube. (p. 126)

central processing unit (CPU) Directs the operation of a computer, performs logical operations and calculations, and stores information. (p. 130)

chat room A network feature that allows two or more users to exchange messages. (p. 141)

chemical energy The energy stored in chemical compounds. (p. 100)

chemical reaction A process in which substances change into new substances with different properties. (p. 100)

circuit breaker A safety device that uses an electromagnet to shut off a circuit when the current becomes too high. (p. 71)

commutator A device that controls the direction of the flow of current through an electric motor. (p. 81)

compass A device with a magnetized needle that can spin freely; a compass needle always points north. (p. 24)

computer An electronic device that stores, processes, and retrieves information. (p. 128)

computer hardware The permanent components of a computer, including the central processing unit and input, output, and memory storage devices. (p. 130)

computer network A group of computers connected by cables or telephone lines that allows people to share information. (p. 138)

computer programmer A person who uses computer languages to write programs, or sets of operation instructions, for computers. (p. 134)

computer software A detailed set of instructions that directs the computer hardware to perform operations on stored information. (p. 134)

computer virus A program that can enter a computer, destroy files, and disable the computer. (p. 140)

conduction A method of charging an object by allowing electrons to flow directly from one object to another object. (p. 49)

conductor A material through which electrons move freely, forming an electric current. (p. 32)

conservation of charge The law that states that charges are neither created nor destroyed. (p. 50)

digital signal Pulses of current used to represent information. (p. 114)

diode A solid-state component that consists of layers of two types of semiconductors. (p. 116)

direct current Current consisting of charges that flow in only one direction in a circuit. (p. 86)

disk drive A device that reads information from a disk or enters information onto a disk for a computer. (p. 132)

diskette A plastic disk that holds information and can be removed from the computer. (p. 132)

dry cell An electrochemical cell in which the electrolyte is a paste. (p. 102)

electrical energy The energy of moving electrical charges. (p. 79)

electrical potential The potential energy per unit of electric charge. (p. 56)

electric charge A property of electrons and protons; electrons carry a negative charge, and protons carry a positive charge. (p. 30)

electric circuit A complete path through which electric charges can flow. (p. 32)

electric current The flow of electric charges through a material. (p. 31)

electric field The field around charged particles that exerts a force on other charged particles. (p. 47)

electric generator A device that converts mechanical energy into electrical energy. (p. 86)

electric motor A device that converts electrical energy to mechanical energy to turn an axle. (p. 80)

electrochemical cell A device that converts chemical energy into electrical energy. (p. 101)

electrode A metal part of an electrochemical cell, which gains or loses electrons. (p. 101)

electrolyte A liquid or paste that conducts electricity. (p. 101)

electromagnet A strong magnet that can be turned on and off; a solenoid with a ferromagnetic core. (p. 39)

electromagnetic induction The process of generating an electric current from the motion of a conductor through a magnetic field. (p. 85)

electromagnetic wave A wave made up of a combination of a changing electric field and changing magnetic field. (p. 123)

electron A negatively charged particle that orbits the nucleus of an atom. (p. 18)

electronics The use of electricity to control, communicate, and process information. (p. 112)

electronic signal A varying electric current that represents information. (p. 113)

electroscope An instrument used to detect electric charge. (p. 53)

element A substance in which all the atoms are alike; one of about 100 basic materials that make up all matter. (p. 18)

encryption A process of coding information so that only the intended user can read it. (p. 140)

energy The ability to move an object some distance. (p. 79)

ferromagnetic material A material that is strongly attracted to a magnet, and which can be made into a magnet. (p. 19)

freeware Software that the author has decided to let others use free of charge. (p. 141)

frequency The number of waves passing a given point each second. (p. 124)

frequency modulation (FM) Changes the frequency of the carrier wave to match the amplitude of the signal. (p. 124)

friction A force that is exerted when two substances are rubbed together; electrons are transferred by the rubbing. (p. 49)

fuse A safety device with a thin metal strip that will melt if too much current passes through a circuit. (p. 70)

galvanometer A device that uses an electromagnet to detect small amounts of current. (p. 79)

grounded Allowing charges to flow directly from the circuit to the ground connection. (p. 69)

hard disk The rigid magnetic metal disk that stays inside a computer and holds information that can be accessed any time the computer is on. (p. 132)

hypothesis A possible explanation for a set of observations or answer to a scientific question; must be testable. (p. 156)

induction A method of electrically charging an object by means of the electric field of another object. (p. 50)

input device A device that feeds data to a CPU; a keyboard is an input device. (p. 130)

insulator A material through which the charges of an electric current are not able to move. (p. 32)

integrated circuit A circuit that has been manufactured on a chip (a tiny slice of semiconductor), which can contain thousands of diodes, transistors, and resistors. (p. 117)

intellectual property A story, poem, computer program, or similar product owned by the author. (p. 141)

Internet An international computer network that links millions of businesses, schools, and research organizations and that has millions of individual users. (p. 139)

lightning rod A metal rod on a building connected to a grounding wire; meant to protect a building from lightning damage. (p. 70)

local area network (LAN) A set of computers connected in one office building or classroom. (p. 139)

magnetic declination The angle between geographic north and the north to which a compass needle points. (p. 26)

magnetic domain A region in which the magnetic fields of all atoms are lined up in the same direction. (p. 19)

magnetic field The region around a magnet where the magnetic force is exerted. (p. 17)

magnetic field lines Lines that map out the magnetic field around a magnet. (p. 17)

magnetic pole The ends of a magnetic object, where the magnetic force is strongest. (p. 15)

magnetism The force of attraction or repulsion of magnetic materials. (p. 15)

magnetosphere The region of Earth's magnetic field shaped by the solar wind. (p. 27)

mechanical energy The energy an object has due to its movement or position. (p. 79)

nonrenewable resource A natural resource that cannot be replaced if used up. (p. 91)

nucleus The core at the center of every atom. (p. 18)

Ohm's law Resistance equals voltage divided by current. (p. 60)

optical disc A disc read by lasers that holds a great amount of information, even more than some hard drives. (p. 133)

output device A device that presents data from a computer; a monitor is an output device. (p. 131)

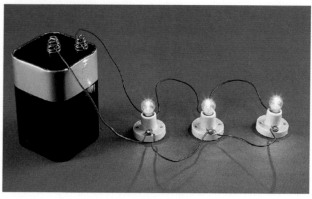

parallel circuit An electric circuit with multiple paths. (p. 66)

permanent magnet A magnet made of material that keeps its magnetism. (p. 20)

potential difference The difference in electrical potential between two places; measured in volts. (p. 57)

power The rate at which one form of energy is converted into another; the unit of power is the Watt; Watts = Volts × Amps. (p. 93)

proton A positively charged particle that is part of an atom's nucleus. (p. 18)

random-access memory (RAM) Temporary storage area for data while the computer is operating. (p. 131)

read-only memory (ROM) Permanent storage area for data in the computer; the CPU can read these data but not change them. (p. 131)

rechargeable battery A battery in which the products of the electrochemical reaction can be turned back into reactants to be reused. (p. 103)

renewable resource A natural resource that can be replaced in nature at a rate close to the rate at which it is used. (p. 91)

resistance The opposition to the movement of electric charges flowing through a material. (p. 34)

resistor A device in an electric circuit that uses electrical energy as it interferes with the flow of electric charge. (p. 34)

semiconductor A material that conducts electricity under certain conditions. (p. 115)

series circuit An electric circuit with a single path. (p. 65)

shareware Software that the author allows others to try out and use for a low fee. (p. 141)

short circuit An electrical connection that allows current to take an unintended path. (p. 68)

slip rings The parts of a generator that rotate with the armature and make contact with the brushes. (p. 87)

solar wind Streams of electrically charged particles flowing at high speeds from the sun; solar wind pushes against Earth's magnetic field and surrounds it. (p. 27)

solenoid A current-carrying coil of wire with many loops that acts as a magnet. (p. 39)

solid-state component The part of a circuit in which a signal is controlled by a solid material. (p. 116)

static discharge The loss of static electricity as electric charges move off an object. (p. 50)

static electricity A buildup of charges on an object. (p. 49)

step-down transformer A transformer that decreases voltage. (p. 95)

step-up transformer A transformer that increases voltage. (p. 95)

superconductor A material that has no electrical resistance. (p. 35)

terminal The part of an electrode above the surface of the electrolyte. (p. 101)

third prong The round prong of a plug which connects the metal shell of an appliance to the safety grounding wire of a building. (p. 69)

transformer A device that increases or decreases voltage. (p. 94)

transistor A solid-state component used to amplify an electronic signal or to switch current on and off. (p. 116)

turbine A circular device with many blades that is turned by water, wind, steam, or tides. (p. 87)

vacuum tube A glass tube from which almost all gases have been removed, and which contains electrodes that control the flow of electrons. (p. 118)

Van Allen belts Two doughnut-shaped regions 1,000–25,000 kilometers above Earth that contain electrons and protons traveling at high speeds. (p. 27)

voltage Potential difference; measured by a voltmeter. (p. 57)

voltage source Creates a potential difference in an electric circuit; batteries and generators are voltage sources. (p. 58)

voltmeter A device used to measure voltage, or potential difference. (p. 60)

wet cell An electrochemical cell in which the electrolyte is a liquid. (p. 102)

wide area network (WAN) A system of computers across large distances, with very large computers that serve as support connections. (p. 139)

World Wide Web Many computers connected over long distances; it allows the displaying and viewing of text, pictures, video, and sound. (p. 140)

Acknowledgments

Staff Credits

The people who made up the **Science Explorer** team—representing design services, editorial, editorial services, electronic publishing technology, manufacturing & inventory planning, marketing, marketing services, market research, online services & multimedia development, production services, product planning, project office, and publishing processes—are listed below.

Carolyn Belanger, Barbara A. Bertell, Suzanne Biron, Peggy Bliss, Peter W. Brooks, Christopher R. Brown, Greg Cantone, Jonathan Cheney, Todd Christy, Lisa J. Clark, Patrick Finbarr Connolly, Edward Cordero, Robert Craton, Patricia Cully, Patricia M. Dambry, Kathleen J. Dempsey, Judy Elgin, Gayle Connolly Fedele, Frederick Fellows, Barbara Foster, Paula Foye, Loree Franz, Donald P. Gagnon Jr., Paul J. Gagnon, Joel Gendler, Elizabeth Good, Robert M. Graham, Kerri Hoar, Joanne Hudson, Linda D. Johnson, Anne Jones, Toby Klang, Carolyn Langley, Russ Lappa, Carolyn Lock, Cheryl Mahan, Dotti Marshall, Meredith Mascola, Jeanne Y. Maurand, Karen McHugh, Eve Melnechuk, Natania Mlawer, Paul W. Murphy, Cindy A. Noftle, Julia F. Osborne, Judi Pinkham, Caroline M. Power, Robin L. Santel, Suzanne J. Schineller, Emily Soltanoff, Kira Thaler-Marbit, Mark Tricca, Diane Walsh, Pearl Weinstein, Merce Wilczek, Helen Young.

Illustration

Albert Molnar: 140
John Edwards and Associates: 26(t), 27, 98
GeoSystems Global Corporation: 26(b)
Martucci Design: 162, 163, 164
Matt Mayerchak: 41, 75, 143, 160, 161
Morgan Cain & Associates: 17, 18, 19, 21, 38, 39, 40, 47, 48, 49, 53, 58, 59, 67, 75, 125, 154
Precision Graphics: 79, 80, 82, 84, 85, 86, 87, 95, 100, 101, 102, 107, 109, 112, 116, 123, 124t, 145
J/B Woolsey Associates: 29, 51, 57, 64, 65, 66, 75, 115, 121, 124b, 127, 130-131, 158

Photography

Photo Research: Toni Michaels
Cover Image: Joseph B. Brignold/The Image Bank

Nature of Science
Page 8, 9t, inset, NASA; **9b,** SPAR Aerospace/SPAR Space Systems; **10-11, 10t,** NASA; **10b,** Courtesy of Ellen Ochoa; **11,** NASA.

Chapter 1
Pages 12-13, Dick Durrance II/The Stock Market; **14t,** Richard Haynes; **14b,** Marcello Bertinetti/Photo Researchers; **15t,** Paul Silverman/ Fundamental Photographs; **15b,** Russ Lappa; **16 both, 17l,** Richard Megna/Fundamental Photographs; **17r,** Phil Degginger/Color-Pic, Inc.; **18 both,** Richard Megna/Fundamental Photographs; **20t,** Russ Lappa; **20b,** Richard Haynes; **22,** Aaron Rezny/The Stock Market; **23 both,** Richard Haynes; **24t,** Russ Lappa; **24b,** Sisse Brimberg/National Geographic Image; **25,** National Geographic Society/NGS Image; **28,** Lionel F. Stevenson/Photo Researchers; **30t,** Russ Lappa; **30b,** Corbis-Bettmann; **31b,** Richard Megna/Fundamental Photographs; **31 all others,** Russ Lappa; **32,** Fred McKinney/FPG International; **33,** Corel Corp.; **33 inset,** Russ Lappa; **34l,** Russ Lappa; **34r,** Richard Megna/Fundamental Photographs; **35,** AT&T Bell Labs/ Science Photo Library/Photo Researchers; **36,** Kevin Cruff/FPG International; **37, 38t,** Richard Haynes; **38b, 39,** Richard Megna/ Fundamental Photographs; **40,** Applied Superconductivity Center at the University of Wisconsin-Madison; **41,** Lionel F. Stevenson/Photo Researchers.

Chapter 2
Pages 44-45, Telegraph Colour Library/FPG International; **46t,** Richard Haynes; **46b,** Mark C. Burnett/Photo Researchers; **49,** Hank Morgan/ Rainbow; **50,** Russ Lappa; **51 both,** Richard Haynes; **52,** Richard Kaylin/TSI; **54, 55,** Richard Haynes; **56t,** Russ Lappa; **56b,** Craig Tuttle, The Stock Market; **57,** Bob Daemmrich/Stock Boston; **59, 60,** Russ Lappa; **61,** M. Antman/The Image Works; **62,** Mark Burnett/Stock Boston; **63,** Richard Haynes; **64,** James Dwyer/Stock Boston; **65, 66, 68,** Russ Lappa; **69t,** Joel Page/AP Wide World Photos; **69b,** Russ Lappa; **70,** Armen Kachaturian/Liaison International; **71l,** Russ Lappa; **71r,** M. Antman/The Image Works; **72,** Ross Harrison Koty/TSI; **73,** Russ Lappa.

Chapter 3
Pages 76-77, John Henley/The Stock Market; **78t,** Russ Lappa; **78b,** Jon Chomitz; **81, 83t,** Russ Lappa; **83b,** Telegraph Colour Library/FPG International; **84,** Richard Haynes; **88t,** Peter Menzel/Stock Boston; **88b,** Martin Rogers/TSI; **88 bkgd,** Peter/Stef Lamberti/TSI; **89t,** Adam Woolfitt/Woodfin Camp & Associates; **89m,** Roger Ball/The Stock Market; **89b,** Stephen J. Krasemann/Photo Researchers; **89 bkgd,** Manfred Gottschalk/Tom Stack & Associates; **91,** Alison Wright/Stock Boston; **92t,** Russ Lappa; **92b,** Frank Siteman/Stock Boston; **94l,** Toni Michaels; **94r,** B. Daemmrich/The Image Works; **95,** Russ Lappa; **96t,** The Granger Collection, NY; **96b,** Corbis-Bettmann; **97t,** The Granger Collection, NY; **97bl, br,** Corbis-Bettmann; **98,** Montes De Oca, Art 1998/FPG International; **99t,** Russ Lappa; **99b,** William Johnson/Stock Boston; **100,** J-L Charmet/ Science Photo Library/Photo Researchers; **103,** Jose Pelaez/The Stock Market; **104t,** David Barnes/TSI; **104b,** Russ Lappa; **105,** Richard Haynes; **106,** David R. Frasier/TSI; **107,** Peter Menzel/Stock Boston.

Chapter 4
Pages 110-111, Tim Davis/Photo Researchers; **113tl,** Bob Daemmrich/ Stock Boston; **113tr,** Bill Horsman/Stock Boston; **113b, 114b,** Russ Lappa; **114 inset,** Dr. Jeremy Burgess/Science Photo Library/Photo Researchers; **115t,** Russ Lappa; **115b,** Russ Lappa/Photo Researchers; **115 inset,** Dr. Jeremy Burgess/Science Photo Library/Photo Researchers; **116 both,** Russ Lappa; **117b,** Manfred Kage/Peter Arnold; **117 inset,** Charles Falco/Photo Researchers; **118,** Ken Whitmore/TSI; **119,** Russ Lappa; **120l,** B. Daemmrich/ The Image Works; **120r,** Camerique/Archive Photos; **122t,** Russ Lappa; **122b,** Richard Pasley/Stock Boston; **123b,** Craig Tuttle/The Stock Market; **123 inset,** Telegraph Colour Library/FPG International; **126,** I. Maier, Jr./The Image Works; **128t,** Richard Haynes; **128b,** L. Dematteis/The Image Works; **129,** Andrew Syred/Science Photo Library/Photo Researchers; **132t,** The Granger Collection, NY; **132b,** Corbis-Bettmann; **133t,** AP/Wide World Photos; **133b,** Camilla Smith/Rainbow; **134,** David Parker/Science Photo Library/Photo Researchers; **135, 136 both, 137,** Russ Lappa; **138,** Sanford/Asliolo/International Stock; **139tl,** AP Photo/Kamran Jebreili; **139tr,** Russ Lappa; **139bl,** Bob Daemmrich/Stock Boston; **139br,** AP Photo/Rick Bethem; **139m,** NASA; **141,** Russ Lappa; **142,** Andrew Oliney & TSI Imaging/TSI.

Interdisciplinary Exploration
Page 146t, Art Resource, NY; **146b,** The Granger Collection, NY; **147 all,** U.S. Dept. of the Interior, National Park Service, Edison National Historic Site; **148-149,** AP/Wide World Photos; **150l, m,** U.S. Dept. of the Interior, National Park Service, Edison National Historic Site; **150br,** Brooks/Brown/Photo Researchers; **151t,** US Geological Survey/Science Photo Library/Photo Researchers; **151bl,** Topham/The Image Works; **151br,** Michael Simpson/FPG International; **151 all others,** Russ Lappa.

Skills Handbook
Page 152, Mike Moreland/Photo Network; **153t,** Foodpix; **153m,** Richard Haynes; **153b,** Russ Lappa; **156,** Richard Haynes; **158,** Ron Kimball; **159,** Renee Lynn/Photo Researchers.